I Ching

I Ching

The Perfect Companion

Gary G. Melyan
&
Wen-kuang Chu

BLACK DOG
& LEVENTHAL
PUBLISHERS
NEW YORK

Copyright © 2003 Black Dog & Leventhal Publishers

Published by
Black Dog & Leventhal Publishers, Inc.
151 West 19th Street
New York, NY 10011

Distributed by
Workman Publishing Company
708 Broadway
New York, NY 10003

Manufactured in China

Cover and interior design by Sheila Hart Design
Cover photograph courtesy Corbis

h g f e d c b a

Text and calligraphy copyright ©1977 Charles E. Tuttle Publishing Co., Inc.
Adapted from *The Pocket I-Ching* by permission of Tuttle Publishing

Library of Congress Cataloging-in-Publication Data
Melyan, Gary G.
I Ching : the perfect companion / by Gary G. Melyan and Wen-Kuang
Chu.-- 1st ed.
     p. cm.
Includes bibliographical references.
ISBN 1-57912-336-8
1. Yi jing. 2. Divination. I. Chu, Wen-kuang, 1934 or 5- II. Title.

PL2464.Z7M45 2003
299.5'1282--dc22
2003014913

Contents

Preface

*T*he growing popularity of the *I-Ching (Book of Changes)* in the West is evidence that rational man, the product of Western tradition, is seeking consolation in ever-increasing numbers in this ancient Chinese oracle book. There are in existence several very good translations and interpretations of this work of philosophy and divination. Nonetheless, the problem of how to interpret and explain the often mysterious and obscure comments that accompany the hexagrams remains.

Those who have seriously studied the *I-Ching* and its tradition can arrive at their own conclusions about what the hexagrams mean in terms of questions directed at them. But those who have not had time or training to become familiar with the intricacies of the *I-Ching* frequently find consulting the oracle a difficult task, one easily leading to a misunderstanding of what the *I-Ching* says. It is to fill the need for a practical and simple introduction to consulting the *I-Ching* as an oracle that Dr. Wenkuang Chu and I have collaborated on this text.

Our goal is to open up the use of the *I-Ching* as an oracle to the non-specialist, giving him a modern context in which to ask his questions.

We also hope that we can introduce to readers some of the implications of this influential philosophical text. The heart of our endeavor is Part Three where we have provided twenty broad categories of human concern. The reader is encouraged to formulate specific questions and address them to these categories following instructions given in "How to Consult the Oracle" of Part One. We have arbitrarily limited our scope to the 20 categories, providing some background information about the hexagrams to enable the reader to determine answers for questions that do not fall within this scope.

That the *I-Ching* is an oracle book of extraordinary effectiveness is something that the Chinese take for granted. The idea that casting yarrow

stalks or coins can lead to the formation of groups of lines which in turn open up an understanding of both present and future circumstances is something difficult for the Western mind to accept. We have not tried to explain just why the key to cosmic influences is hidden in the hexagrams. We can do no more than offer our interpretation of the hexagrams, hoping that use of our text in divination will make believers out of skeptics.

People in many Oriental communities use handbooks similar to this one and have found their use very effective. We hope that our readers will also find this approach to the *I-Ching* helpful in their daily lives.

We are very grateful to Liu Ta-yung for the calligraphy that introduces each trigram and hexagram.

Gary G. Melyan

Part
One

What Is the *I-Ching*?

One of the five Confucian Classics, the *I-Ching*, or as it is commonly translated, the *Book of Changes*, is an oracle book, a philosophy, and a work of art. It has added immeasurable depth to Chinese culture and is doing the same now for Western culture.

The *I-Ching* is composed of 64 Hexagrams made up of six broken or solid (unbroken) lines, texts, and commentaries. The basic symbolic unit is a trigram. The maximum number of trigrams formed by various combinations of three lines, either solid ——— or broken— — , is eight. By combining individual trigrams the hexagram is formed, the total possible being 64.

These lines, trigrams, and hexagrams symbolize the forces of action and change and all the phenomena of the universe. The lines are of two kinds: the broken, representing the *yin* force, and the solid, representing the *yang* force. The yin force refers to the negative, passive, weak, and destructive. It is docile and female. The yang force refers to the positive, active, strong, and constructive. It is virile and male. Together in groups of six the lines symbolize all possible situations, forms of change,

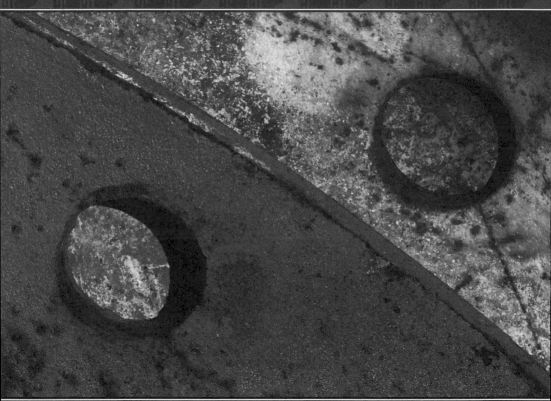

possibilities, and institutions. The underlying idea is that the two forces are constantly interacting, producing change, and that things are forever interfused and intermingled. In simple terms this perpetual constant is the constant of change. The universe so represented is controlled by a natural operation of forces which can be determined and predicted objectively.

The origins of the work lie in the desire to predict the future based on wisdom symbolically embodied in the hexagrams. The word that is translated into English from the Chinese as change is *i* 易 , pronounced *ee*. Basically *i* has three meanings: 1) ease and simplicity in contrast to what is difficult; 2) transformation, alternation, or change; 3) firm and quiet in contrast to what is endangered, hence invariability. These meanings serve as undertones throughout the work.

The 64 Hexagrams are followed by two texts and commentaries. The total is what we today call the *I-Ching*. We shall use this name rather than the translated title in our text.

History

*T*radition ascribes the basic linear complexes of the book, the Eight Trigrams, to the legendary cultural hero Fu Hsi. He is said to have investigated all the phenomena in the universe and discovered a commonality of laws or patterns governing everything. These phenomena and laws were inductively symbolized by the Eight Trigrams. Tradition is split as to the attribution of the 64 Hexagrams, some attributing them to

Fu Hsi and others to King Wen (c. 1171–1122 B.C.), the father of the founder of the Chou dynasty (1111–249 B.C.). Regardless of the authenticity of these attributions, it is certain that the idea of the line groups and of the divided and solid lines goes back to remote antiquity.

Our present text is said to be a revision of two earlier works of which nothing reliable remains. The first is called the *Lien Shan*, "Mountains Standing Together," and is placed in the Hsia dynasty (c. 2183–1752 B.C.). The other, used in the Shang dynasty (1751–1112 B.C.), is called *Kuei Tsang*, "Reverting to the Hidden." We only know the names of these books and that their arrangement and names of the hexagrams were different.

The old name of the work that comes down to us is *Chou I*; Chou is the name of the dynasty whose founders played such an important role in shaping the work. It is attributed either to King Wen or his son, the Duke of Chou. It is not our concern here to discuss which parts of the text stemmed from which historical figure. It is important only to note that the text dates back to the early Chou period and that the Chou influence gave the work an emphasis on human affairs.

The latest part of the book is the commentary, commonly called the Ten Wings, and is ascribed to Confucius, although this attribution has been challenged by modern scholars. Most probably the Ten Wings are a product of many hands over a long period of time, from the fifth or sixth century to the third or fourth century B.C. However, it is true that Confucius did study the hexagrams and texts intensively and seriously in his old age. Thus the commentaries doubtlessly bear the stamp of his keen intelligence, his judgments and observations influencing later writers of commentaries whether they were Confucian disciples or not.

Fate too played a role in pushing the *I-Ching* to the forefront of intellectual interest. It was one of the few works to escape the great book burning of 213 B.C. initiated by Ch'in Shih Huang Ti, the first emperor of China. As a result scholars took up the *I-Ching* with great enthusiasm, feeling that it was the last tool of their profession. They contributed an enormous amount of heterogeneous material coming from such diverse schools as the Taoists and the natural philosophers. The rich and varied commentary that surrounds the work originated under these circumstances and forms the *I-Ching* tradition.

Also fusing with the tradition of the hexagrams were early schools of Chinese astronomy and astrology with such concepts as the Five Elements (Metal, Wood, Water, Fire, and Earth), the Ten Celestial Stems, and the Twelve Zodiacal Places (also known as the Twelve Horary Characters or Terrestrial Branches). Matched with the 64 Hexagrams, these concepts formed the base for *I-Ching* divination from the Han dynasty (B.C. 206–220 A.D.) onward. Many schools of thought used the *I-Ching* to predict great events of state and to explain the development of history—not only the Confucianists. This made the *I-Ching* broader in use and influence than other Chinese classical works and guarantees it a prominent, living position throughout history.

Composition of the Book

he 64 Hexagrams are followed by two texts and commentaries. The texts are the *Kua Tz'u*, or explanation of the entire hexagram text, and the *Yao Tz'u*, or explanation of the component lines. There are seven commentaries. First is the *T'uan Chuan*, which is the commentary on the decision that uses the structure of the individual hexagrams to explain the judgments belonging to them, i.e., the commentary on the *Kua Tz'u*. Then there is the *Hsiang Chuan* or "Commentary on the Images." By studying the images suggested by the primary trigrams, this commentary arrives at an abstract meaning for the hexagram. (It also appends explanations to the individual lines.) Next is the *Wen Yen* or "Commentary on Words of the Text."

Preserved for us is commentary on the first two hexagrams, emphasizing their philosophical meaning.

The following layer of text is the *Tza Kua* or "Miscellaneous Notes on the Hexagrams," which briefly defines the names of the hexagrams. The subsequent layer is the *Hsü Kua* or "Sequence of Hexagrams," which is the basis for our present order of hexagrams. It is followed by the *Shuo Kua* or "Discussion of the Trigrams," which interprets the Eight Trigrams and the symbolic values represented by each.

Lastly there is the *Hsi Tz'u*, "Appended Judgments," which gives a general introduction to the text as a whole and contains pronouncements about the *I-Ching* made by the Confucian School—some probably emanating from Confucius himself. The *T'uan Chuan*, *Hsiang Chuan*, and *Hsi Tz'u* are each in two parts and, with the rest of the commentaries, form the Ten Wings.

How to Consult the Oracle

he *Book of Changes* is an oracle book—that is, a system of ideas, natural laws, and images from which one can obtain an answer to a question about what is to come if the question is worded precisely. There are two methods used to construct hexagrams from which the answers are interpreted. One is to obtain the auguries by the manipulation of fifty yarrow (or milfoil) stalks. Though this method is the oldest—the practice of using the stalks came about because they grew wild in the place which in ancient times was used for sacred rituals—we will not introduce it. The second method is far easier and much more convenient. This is the method of tossing coins.

Traditionally the Chinese used copper coins with holes in the middle, blank on one side and inscribed on the other. For our purposes any coin will do.

Tossing Coins

ake three of the same type of coin and arbitrarily determine one side as *yang* and the other as *yin*. Coins with a head and tail can conveniently be *yang* and *yin* respectively. After composing oneself and having asked the specific question, shake the coins well and throw them to build the bottom line of the hexagram. Continue in this manner until six lines are constructed, starting from the bottom and building upward.

Four possible lines can be determined from throwing the coins. If all three coins are heads (or *yang*), the line is an old or changing *yang* line. Likewise if all three coins are tails (or *yin*), the resulting line will be an old or changing *yin* line. If there is one head (*yang*) and two tails (*yin*), the line is a young or unchanging *yang* line. Contrarily, one tail (*yin*) and two heads (*yang*) will produce a young or unchanging *yin* line.

Traditionally the inscription side was given the number value 2 and functioned as the *yin*. The blank side had the value of 3 and functioned as the *yang*. In *I-Ching* terminology a six when referring to a line meant an old, changing *yin* line while a nine meant an old, changing *yang* line. Three blank sides, or heads, result in the number nine. Three inscribed sides, or tails, result in the number six. The other totals are eight for two blank or head sides plus an inscribed or tail side and seven for two inscribed or tail sides plus one blank or head side. A line with a total eight is a young *yin* and seven is young *yang*.

A changing or old line means that when the hexagram is formed that particular line will be changed into its opposite. Hence, if it is *yin* it will become *yang* and vice versa. The first hexagram determined will indicate the pres-

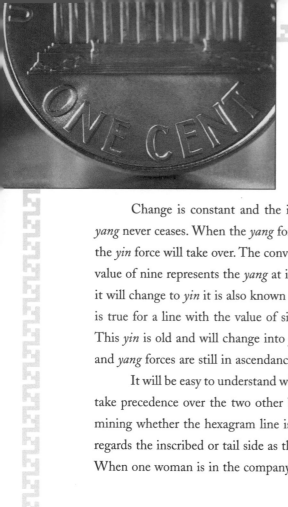

ent situation. Converting all changing lines to their opposites will
result in a second hexagram, the
hexagram which points to the
future situation.

Change is constant and the interaction between the *yin* and the
yang never ceases. When the *yang* force reaches its zenith it will fade and
the *yin* force will take over. The converse is also true. Thus a line with the
value of nine represents the *yang* at its zenith and is called the old. Since
it will change to *yin* it is also known as the changing *yang* line. The same
is true for a line with the value of six, representing the *yin* at its zenith.
This *yin* is old and will change into *yang*. In the other two lines, the *yin*
and *yang* forces are still in ascendancy, so there is no change.

It will be easy to understand why one inscribed or tail (*yin*) side will
take precedence over the two other blank or head (*yang*) sides in determining whether the hexagram line is *yin* (broken) or *yang* (solid), if one
regards the inscribed or tail side as the female and the other as the male.
When one woman is in the company of two men, she controls the situa-

tion. Likewise, two women in the company of one man are under his control. Thus, the one blank or head coin will take precedence over the others and the line determined by the throw will be *yang*.

The following list will simplify the interpretation of lines.

H = *Head or blank side* = 3
T = *Tail or inscribed side* = 2

H + H + H = 9 = Changing yang line
(solid line changing into broken)

T + T + T = 6 = Changing yin line
(broken line changing into solid)

H + T + T = 7 = Young yang line
(solid)

T + H + H = 8 = Young yin line
(broken)

A changing *yang* line is written ——◯—— and a changing *yin* line is written ——✕—— . A young *yin* is written —— —— and a young *yang* line is written ———— . When throwing for the hexagram it is a good idea to keep a record of the lines as you build the hexagram. Any method convenient will do. For illustration here we will use these time-honored symbols for the lines.

Example: On the first toss the coins come up one *yang* and two *yin* (one blank or head side and two inscribed or tail sides). The number value is seven and is written ———— . The second toss results in three *yin* (all inscribed or tails). The number value is six and is written ——✕—— . The third toss results in one *yin* and two *yang* (one inscribed or tail side and two blank or head sides). The number value is eight and is written —— —— . The fourth toss is the same as the third, —— —— . The fifth toss results in three *yang* (all three coins blank or head). The number value is nine and is written ——◯—— . The sixth and last toss comes up the same as the first and is written ———— . The hexagram formed is No. 42 *I* (Increase). This is the starting situation.

6 ————
5 ——◯——
4 —— ——
3 —— ——
2 ——✕——
1 ————

If lines two and five, counting from the bottom, are changed, the resulting hexagram will give the future situation. In this case an old *yin* line is changed to a *yang* and an old *yang* line is changed into a *yin*. This is hexagram No. 41 *Sun* (Decrease). Thus the situation at the time of the throwing is represented by Increase and all this hexagram symbolizes while future developments will go in accord with what Decrease symbolizes. If no changing lines appear, then the situation covered by the hexagram in question will provide you with the answer to your question.

This method of tossing coins to build hexagrams is the easiest and most popular method of consulting the oracle. The difficulty in consulting the oracle lies in the problem of how to interpret the hexagram and corresponding texts. Masters combine their profound knowledge of the *I-Ching* and its tradition with the principles of the Five Elements, Twelve Zodiacal Places, and Ten Celestial Stems. Interpretation has been and still is the key to accurate use of the oracle. Our introduction provides twenty basic situations with answers or the basics necessary for arriving at an answer. Also given are the characteristics of the Eight Trigrams and the 64 Hexagrams. Studying these linear complexes will provide an understanding of the nature of their symbolic values.

The Question
and Interpretation

First decide on your question. The more specific you make it the better. For instance, to ask "Will I get rich?" is too hazy. It is better to ask "Will I succeed in X business?" or "Will I get wealthy by doing X business?" Also, "either-or" questions are to be avoided. To ask whether it is better to go east or west is not the right kind of question. It is better to ask "What will happen if I go east?" A few sample questions show the precise frame needed.

> *If X is done, what will be the result?*
> *In X situation, is it wise to proceed with project Y?*
> *In how many days (weeks, months, years) will it be possible to accomplish X?*

Perhaps the most common question asked by *I-Ching* users is whether a certain endeavor or situation will turn out favorably or not. "Is it favorable for me to do X?" The answers looked for in the Chinese are *chi* 吉 or *li* 利, both meaning favorable, auspicious and propitious, and *hsiung* 兇, meaning unfavorable or adverse.

It is best to first calm yourself, concentrate on the question, and then throw the coins. When the hexagram is built, turn to the appropriate hexagram number in Part Three after finding its number in the chart on page 39. Read the general explanation of the hexagram and the fortune and then try to fit your question into one of the remaining 19 categories. Your question may fit into more than one category. In the instance where it does not fit under any of the categories, you can determine an answer by checking the two component trigrams in Part Two and carefully reading the characteristics of the hexagram. If changing lines are present in your hexagram, be sure to consult both the original and the resulting hexagrams, remembering that the former refers to the present while the latter refers to possibilities in the future.

In addition to the upper and lower trigrams, the hexagrams also contain two "inner" or "nuclear" trigrams. These too are important in interpreting answers. The easiest way to show these trigrams is by diagram.

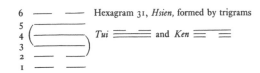

6 — — Hexagram 31, *Hsien,* formed by trigrams
5
4 (=====) *Tui* ===== and *Ken* == ==
3
2 — —
1 — —

The nuclear trigrams are lines two, three, and four (counting from the bottom) forming trigram *Sun* ===== and lines three, four, and five forming trigram *Ch'ien* =====. These two trigrams combined form Hexagram 44, *Kuo* (Coming to meet). Thus, in addition to looking at trigrams *Tui* ===== and *Ken* == ==, which are the component parts of Hexagram 31, and at the hexagram itself, one must keep in mind all meanings, images, and

associations of the two nuclear trigrams and the resulting hexagram. In this case the resulting hexagram *Kuo* has the meaning of intercourse or contact between man and woman, giving hexagram *Hsien* the meaning of contact between the sexes. For marriage, then, *Hsien* is auspicious.

It is hoped that these categories will be sufficient for your purposes. When they are not, remember to look also at the nuclear trigrams when determining your answer.

There is one more thing to remember. Tradition maintains that the answers provided by the hexagrams and the subsequent interpretation are accurate only if the user is calm and collected when consulting the oracle, when his life is not extremely reckless, and when no ulterior motives, such as desire for fast money, exist. The number of men and women who frequently use the *I-Ching* is large and growing. This number even includes the distinguished Chinese Nobel Prize laureate physicists Tsung Tso-lee and Chen Ning-yang (1957) and the Japanese physicist Hideki Yukawa, who won the Nobel Prize for physics in 1947. All three have written that they regularly consult the *I-Ching* at each step of their research.

Further Reading

his book is an introduction. After familiarity is gained the reader will want to go beyond our scope. Two English translations of the *I-Ching* are readily available. James Legge, the translator of numerous Chinese classics, completed his rendering of the *I-Ching* into English in 1882. Originally called "The *Yi-King*" and published as vol. 16 of The Sacred Books of the East (Oxford, Clarendon Press, 1882), Legge's work was reprinted by University Books, New Hyde Park, New York, 1964, with an "Introduction and Study Guide" by Ch'u Chai and Winberg Chai. The great German Sinologist Richard Wilhelm's translation of the *I-Ching* has been rendered into English by Cary F. Baynes. It was first published in two volumes in New York by Pantheon Books, 1950. Princeton University Press has republished it as volume XXIX of their Bollingen Series. Wilhelm's son Hellmut, a great Sinologist in his own right, has provided an excellent general survey of the *I-Ching* in his *Change: Eight Lectures on The I-Ching*, translated from the German by Cary F. Baynes (New York, Pantheon Books, 1960).

Starting with these works the enthusiast may delve into the *I-Ching*, going far deeper than we do here.

Hexagram-Finding Key

Upper Trigram

Lower Trigram	Ch'ien	K'un	Chen	K'an	Ken	Sun	Li	Tui
Ch'ien	1	11	34	5	26	9	14	43
K'un	12	2	16	8	23	20	35	45
Chen	25	24	51	3	27	42	21	17
K'an	6	7	40	29	4	59	64	47
Ken	33	15	62	39	52	53	56	31
Sun	44	46	32	48	18	57	50	28
Li	13	36	55	63	22	37	30	49
Tui	10	19	54	60	41	61	38	58

Part
Two

乾坤震坎

The Eight Trigrams

艮巽離兌

Trigram in *I-Ching* terminology refers to a three-line configuration. The lines are of two kinds, solid ——— and broken — —. The total possible combinations of these lines is eight. The lines when combined to form trigrams take on a broad spectrum of symbolic meaning. In turn, the eight trigrams are combined to form 64 six-line configurations known as hexagrams. For divination purposes the hexagram is all important, but no adequate interpretation of the meaning of the hexagram is possible without an understanding of its component parts.

The order of information about the trigrams is as follows: 1) Wade-Giles system of romanization for pronunciation, the standard romanized name; 2) pronunciation of the trigram in *pinyin*, the romanization system selected for national usage by the People's Republic of China; 3) Richard Wilhelm's translation of the trigram; 4) the trigram itself; and 5) the Chinese character for the trigram.

The human and natural affairs and phenomena associated with each of the eight trigrams follow.

Made up of three solid lines, this trigram symbolizes heaven and thus it is noble, lofty, and firm. It is light as opposed to dark. It also symbolizes the strong, the expansive, and the masculine. It is creative and active, perpetually moving, never stopping. Opposites confront each other in *Chi'en* and it is the time for decisive battles to be fought. *Chi'en* is energy while *K'un*, the next trigram and virtual opposite, is form.

People: Rulers, presidents, sovereigns, dictators, leaders, sages, founders of a religion, popes, church elders, prime ministers, board chairmen, military commanders, fathers, husbands, and old men.

Parts of the body: The head, face, lungs, pleura.

Sicknesses: Headaches, constipation, pulmonary diseases, broken bones, fevers, and swelling.

Places: Palaces, official halls, offices, temples, shrines, churches, theaters, schools, military encampments, markets, mountains, walls and fortifications, observation platforms, race tracks, stadiums, and athletic fields.

Occupations: Government service, the military, businesses concerned with machinery, sports equipment, precious metals, fruit, and watches or clocks.

Articles: Precious stones and metals, watches and clocks, stamps and chops (an official seal, stamp, or permit in India and China), automobiles, streetcars, bicycles, sewing machines, machine guns, overcoats, hats, umbrellas, mosquito nets, purses, mouth covers, clothing, cloth wrappers, and mail boxes.

Food: Rice, beans, canned goods, and fresh fruits.

Animals: Horses, dragons, tigers, and lions.

Plants: The chrysanthemum, fresh fruits, and herbs.

Season: Late autumn or early winter, the time when opposites meet.

Weather: Clear, cold.

Color: Strong red.

Direction: Northwest.

Miscellaneous: Round shapes, abundance or fullness, rapid advancements, charity or donations, happiness or gratification, just before midnight, bravery and boldness, determination, wealth and high position, honor, pride, luxury, cold, ice, the color white, and acrid taste.

Formed by three broken lines, *K'un* stands for the earth, a great plain able to grow a myriad of things. Hence it contains the meaning of mother. People trample and spit on the ground, yet it toils without rest. Therefore, it has the meanings of being gentle and yielding, durable, devoted, and toiling. The earth is formed by fine particles collected together and thus the trigram means mass or the majority. The heaven is lofty, solitary, and noble. The earth is lowly, humble, and yielding; hence *K'un* also means poor, lowly, and inferior. It is passive rather than active and dark as opposed to light. It is the time when peaceful labor is performed.

People: The people, the multitude, groups, mothers, old women, wives, workers, the industrious, handymen, the poverty-stricken, the incapable, and the ignorant.

Parts of the body: The spleen, stomach, and abdomen.

Sicknesses: Diseases in the digestive tract.

Places: Fields, farms, empty lands, uncultivated wilds, and slum areas.

Occupations: Obstetrics, doctors treating gastrointestinal disorders, those who work with antiques or curios.

Articles: Cotton cloth, trousers, pants, chair cushions, sheets, mats, mattresses, square-shaped items, chessboards, boxes, suitcases, kettles, and carriages. As the earth is the base for all things, everything belonging to the bottom level is symbolized here.

Food: Powdered or ground food, sweet potatoes, taro, wheat, sugar, desserts or snacks.

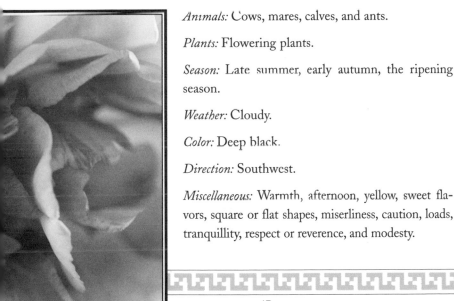

Animals: Cows, mares, calves, and ants.

Plants: Flowering plants.

Season: Late summer, early autumn, the ripening season.

Weather: Cloudy.

Color: Deep black.

Direction: Southwest.

Miscellaneous: Warmth, afternoon, yellow, sweet flavors, square or flat shapes, miserliness, caution, loads, tranquillity, respect or reverence, and modesty.

Chen symbolizes the launching of energy and movement. It is the arousing, the initiator of life. And it is speed. Of the directions, *Chen* represents the east. When the sun rises in the east of vitality and vigor appears throughout the earth. Thus it is the time of blossoming, of expansion, and of the beginning of new things. New ventures and occupations are suggested. *Chen* also stands for thunder and earthquakes, and thus has the meaning of shocking or startling.

The bottom line is a *yang* line, a light rather than dark line. Its position there makes this one of the three light trigrams symbolizing the three sons.

People: Princes, famous people, eldest sons, youths, the nouveaux riches, newly risen people.

Parts of the body: Feet, liver, throat.

Sicknesses: Hysteria, spasms, convulsions and the like, phobias, liver and foot ailments, and disorders of the nervous system.

Places: Forests, houses or buildings being remodeled or repaired, music or concert halls, telecommunications offices, broadcast stations, lecture halls, auditoriums, power stations, electric companies, and gunpowder factories.

Occupations: Switchboard operators, telephone and telegraph operators, technicians, engineers, musicians, broadcast personnel or announcers, those working in record shops and music stores, and those engaged in businesses involving arms and munitions.

Articles: Firecrackers, fireworks, guns, rifles, rockets, gunpowder, pianos, organs, trumpets, records, clarinets, record players, stringed musical instruments, flutes, drums, guitars, bells, gongs, harmonicas, telephones.

Food: Green vegetables, bean sprouts, pomelos, grapefruits, lemons, bamboo shoots, and plums.

Animals: Eagles, swallows, canaries, larks, cicadas, bees, crickets, centipedes, spiders, and frogs.

Plants: Trees, green vegetables, bamboo, freshly sprouting or blossoming plants.

Season: Spring.

Weather: Clear, thunder, storms.

Color: Green or the color of something young or new.

Direction: East.

Miscellaneous: Decision, struggle and determination, frivolousness, sourness, sunrise, flying, freshness, lectures, and satellite launching.

The second light trigram, the yang line coming in the middle, *K'an* symbolizes water. Rain falls from the sky, striking against rocks and cliffs. Sometimes it falls on trees and grass. Drop by drop it comes together forming a trickle, then a stream, then a river, and finally pours into an ocean. Therefore, *K'an* connotes trouble, danger, toil, sadness, and floods. It also means to accumulate or gather together, starting from the small and achieving the large.

Water descends from a higher elevation to a lower one. Thus *K'an* suggests the abysmal, lowness, the underground, and the low-lying. In everyday life it means poverty, want, worries, and sickness. It is the piercing and the penetrating. Yet there is a positive side—perseverance when confronted with danger and endurance in the face of toil will lead to success.

People: Middle sons or second sons, middle-aged men, bandits, thieves, "bad guys," evildoers, the sick, the blind, those with cares and woes, toilers, adulteresses, paramours, nymphomaniacs or sex maniacs, the dead.

Parts of the body: Ears, the anus, nostrils, the reproductive organs, the blood, the kidneys, sweat, and tears.

Sicknesses: Kidney ailments, earaches, venereal disease, hemorrhoids, and alcoholism.

Places: Large rivers, banquet or meeting halls, funeral parlors, hospitals, convalescent homes, wells, baths, brothels, caves, cold places, waterworks installations, aquariums, firehouses, waterfalls, hot springs.

Occupations: Bartender, bathhouse attendant, those working in a dye shop, brothel, or milkstand, prostitutes, and fishermen.

Articles: Waistbands, ink, oil, coal tar, varnish or lacquer, and medicine.

Food: Wine, soup, drinks, salt, soy sauce, seaweed, lotus roots, and sashimi (raw fish).

Animals: The fox, rats, bats, boars.

Plants: Plums, daffodils, narcissus, algae, hard wood.

Season: Winter.

Weather: Rainy, floods, heavy rains or downpours, cold, cloudy and dark.

Color: Blood red and black.

Direction: North.

Miscellaneous: Risks, dangers, cunning, trickery, salty, wisdom and intelligence, worries, thoughts, hidden crime and unrevealed guilt, social and sexual intercourse, theft, the moon, midnight, the melancholic and sick in spirit.

The third of the light trigrams, the *yang* line being on top, *Ken* symbolizes mountains. As mountains do not move and are stationary, *Ken* connotes motionlessness, quietude, stopping, resting, being static, and cessation. As mountains are formed by piling up small particles of earth, *Ken* also means accumulation. The idea of completion has come to be attached to this trigram because *Ken* in plants is the fruit, meaning the completion of the plant.

People: Youngest sons, youths, the overweight, the hunchbacked (those with abnormal curvature of the spine), the greedy, the lazy, those who hoard wealth, and prisoners or convicts.

Parts of the body: The back, waist, nose, hands, fingers, joints, and fleshy tumors.

Sicknesses: Side aches, arthritis, illnesses caused by fatigue, and nasal inflammations.

Places: Buildings, doors, gates, paths, walls, graves, hotels, garages, dikes, stairs, high stages or platforms.

Occupations: Monks, Taoist practitioners, the clergy (priests, ministers, rabbis, etc.), and the restaurant business.

Articles: Things stored up or piled together, screens, tables, and building blocks.

Food: Preserved foods, sweets.

Animals: Dogs, rats, bulls, oxen, tigers.

Plants: Fruits (grown on trees).

Season: Late winter to early spring.

Weather: Cloudy, weather as if about to change.

Color: Dark yellow.

Direction: Northeast.

Miscellaneous: Sweetness, the twilight (night turning into day), tardiness, slowness, stubbornness, sincerity or candor, independence, loftiness, frugality, and saving.

6

SUN

sun

Gentle

The preceding three trigrams were the light and the three sons. The remaining three trigrams are the dark and the three daughters. The dark line (the *yin* or broken line) is on the bottom in *Sun*, in the middle in the seventh, and on top in the eighth and final trigram.

The eldest daughter, *Sun* symbolizes the wind. As the wind blows in from afar, it connotes distance, remoteness, and distant places. The wind reaches everywhere, hence its attribute is penetration. The wind stirs the air and keeps it flowing; thus *Sun* also means interflow or an intermediary role. Interflow and interaction easily suggest marriage (interaction between men and women), commerce and trade (interflow of goods), and credit. *Sun* is also the tall tree and wood.

It characterizes persevering labor and also vehemence. In general it suggests purity, completeness, and quiet contemplation. But it also can mean indecision.

People: Businessmen, travelers, eldest daughters, and sisters.

Parts of the body: Buttocks, thighs, elbows, the intestines, nerves, digestive tract, eyes.

Sicknesses: Colds, digestive ailments, an upset stomach, and diseases of the stomach and bowels.

Occupations: Those engaged in moving and transport, shipping, the construction industry and carpentry, as well as guides, plasterers, and bricklayers.

Articles: String, thread, wire, rope, tables, lumber, railroads, pencils, matches, drawers, swings, postal items, electric fans, and bellows.

Food: Noodles (wheat), onions, leeks, garlic, greens.

Animals: The cock, chickens, cranes, snakes, earthworms, and the chi-lin (in Chinese mythology, a supernatural animal resembling a deer; also known as the unicorn).

Plants: Grass, willows, reeds and rushes, the lily, the calamus.

Season: Between late spring and early summer.

Weather: Windy and cloudy.

Color: White.

Direction: Southeast.

Miscellaneous: Clouds, forenoon (from 7 A.M. to 11 A.M., the time of hard work), green, orderly or neat appearance, length and height, obedience, adjustments, marriage arrangements, travel, dismissal or disbanding, distant or remote places, and hesitation.

The second dark trigram, the second or middle daughter, symbolizes the sun and fire. From this a host of associations is created—brightness, brilliance, beauty, ferocity, disasters such as fires, dryness, and separation. *Li* also means dangerous weapons and fighting. This light-giving trigram also means perception.

People: Middle daughters, middle-aged women, beauties, wise and intelligent people.

Parts of the body: Eyes, heart, the spirit (energy), breasts, blood.

Sicknesses: Eye diseases, mental illness, high fevers, heart ailments, headaches.

Places: Police stations, lighthouses, fire departments, department stores, theaters, schools, courthouses, downtown, battlefields, scenes of fires.

Occupations: Writers, artists, artisans, eye doctors, the police, war correspondents, soldiers, and those in the munitions, department store, barber shop, beauty parlor, and bookstore businesses.

Articles: Paintings, works of calligraphy, books, ornaments and decorations, electric lights, candles, lamps, pots, kettles, stocks, checks, bonds, armor, weapons.

Food: Dry foods, turtles, oysters, shelled seafood (clams and the like), crabs, beautifully arranged or colored foods.

Animals: Pheasants, chicks, goldfish, fireflies, crabs, lobsters, turtles, snails, mussels, tortoises, and mollusks.

Plants: The crepe myrtle, maples, the beefsteak plant (Perilla nankinensis), watermelons, and red colored plants.

Season: Summer.

Weather: Clear, warm, hot day; droughts.

Color: Red and purple.

Direction: South.

Miscellaneous: Noon, brightness, lightning, radicalness, violence, nervousness, impulsiveness, intelligence, passion, enthusiasm, electricity, rainbows, bitter taste.

The last dark trigram is the youngest daughter, the symbol of young girls, of joy, delight, and gaiety. *Tui* is the marsh, a low-lying place that connotes insufficiency, incompleteness, inadequacy, defectiveness, and things that are concave or indented. Associated with the trigram are reflection, enticement, and destruction or ruin. As *Tui* means the pleasurable and the happy (food, drink, and money), the opposite idea is suggested. Danger can result from an excess of pleasure.

People: Youngest daughters, young girls, young ladies, girl friends, female stars or celebrities, female vocalists, bar girls, hostesses, prostitutes, concubines, sorceresses, witches, the incompetent or feeble.

Articles: Knives, blades, money, and musical instruments.

Parts of the body: Mouth, lungs, respiratory organs, the chest, and teeth.

Sicknesses: Afflictions of the mouth cavity and illnesses in the chest and breast region.

Places: Valleys, ponds, marshes, low-lying ground, hollows, ditches, riversides, places where water is accumulated or deep lakes, bars, taverns, beverage shops, brothel or prostitution districts.

Occupations: Lawyers, lecturers, and those involved in monetary concerns or drinking establishments.

Food: Coffee, tea, wine, alcohol, mutton, bird meat.

Animals: Sheep, birds, monkeys.

Plants: Autumn plants, Chinese bellflowers, magnolias, plants with a peppery, spicy, or hot taste such as ginger and red pepper, and plants growing beside marshes, swamps, and lakes.

Season: Autumn.

Weather: Rainy

Color: White and golden color.

Direction: West

Miscellaneous: Hot, spicy, or peppery taste, evening or twilight, singing and songs, arguments, damage or destruction, setbacks or failures, dew, snow, gentleness, happiness, a consuming interest or hobby, laughter, a "big mouth," lawsuits or litigation, sexual passion or lust, speech.

Part
Three

The 64 Hexagrams: explanation and practical application in divination

PRIMARY
NUCLEAR

$Upper$ $\begin{cases} 6 \\ 5 \\ 4 \end{cases}$ ———————— ⎤
———————— |— *Above*
———————— ⎦

$Lower$ $\begin{cases} 3 \\ 2 \\ 1 \end{cases}$ ———————— ⎤
———————— |— *Below*
———————— ⎦

*E*ach of the following 64 Hexagrams is given a brief explanation in terms of symbolic representation of phenomena and actual application in divination. If the reader thoroughly familiarizes himself with the ideas in this section, he will naturally be able to expand use of the hexagrams beyond the scope of the phenomena listed below. The key to utilizing the hexagrams lies in the understanding of the fundamental concepts embodied in them.

The hexagrams show one's position in time and implications of future potentialities. They provide the basis for correct action in a given situation.

In applying the hexagrams it is best to remember the pointers on use mentioned in Part One (pages 32–35).

The order of information about the hexagrams is as follows: 1) hexagram number, 2), the hexagram itself, 3) pronunciation in the standard Wade-Giles romanization system, 4) pronunciation in the *pinyin* system, 5) Richard Wilhelm's translation of the hexagram, and 6) the corresponding Chinese character(s) for the hexagram.

The primary and nuclear trigrams of each hexagram are listed for the convenience of the reader. Counting from the bottom, lines 1, 2, 3 form the lower trigram, and lines 4, 5, 6 form the upper trigram. The nuclear trigrams are formed by lines 2, 3, 4 (the below) and lines 3, 4, 5 (the above).

HEXAGRAM 1

CH'IEN

qian

The creative

	Primary	Upper	*Ch'ien*	*Creative*
		Lower	*Ch'ien*	*Creative*
	Nuclear	Above	*Ch'ien*	*Creative*
		Below	*Ch'ien*	*Creative*

Ch'ien symbolizes heaven and the creative power. All lines are solid or *yang*, meaning that all associated trigrams, both primary and nuclear, are *Ch'ien*. It is the zenith of the *yang* force. *Ch'ien* is light, strong and active, suggesting action and perseverance. By extension, *Ch'ien* stands for the universe which is endlessly changing. Thus *Ch'ien* also implies emulation of the way of heaven, of diligence throughout the day, and of ceaseless exertion and hard work. The *I-Ching* seeks to apply the principles of heaven and earth to human conduct and affairs. *Ch'ien* stands for the way of heaven and the following hexagram, *K'un*, elucidates the way of the earth. The two, heaven and earth, stand at the beginning of the *I-Ching*.

Ch'ien symbolizes the prosperity of all things, strong and flourishing. But in the midst of the most extreme *yang*, *yin* is bound to come into existence. Therefore, caution is advised. Take heed to avoid the unexpected and accidental.

THE FORTUNE

Everything is according to plans or expectations. Prosperity and the realization of fame and fortune. Overcomplacency, self-satisfaction, and arrogance or an overbearing manner will, however, summon misfortune. Accordingly, be careful, cautious, and thoughtful in doing things.

Wish: Can be attained. But be open and humble in doing things.

Marriage: The man will make a good husband. Setting sights too high will result in failure.

Love: Success is possible. But if both sides are selfish, the result will be a breaking off of the friendship.

Family: Happy and prosperous. Arrogance and waste will, however, lead to ruin.

Children: Healthy, blessed with happiness and ability, but they must not be spoiled while growing up. More boys than girls. Pregnancy: boy.

Capital loan: No problem, but you must carefully handle the whole process.

Business: You will earn a profit, but it is not fitting to try to enlarge upon that profit.

Stock market: Prices are high now but will soon drop; sell.

Life span: A healthy and long life. Attention must be placed on the daily regimen, otherwise your health will be affected. Special care must be given to chest and head-related illnesses or diseases.

Sickness: Condition relatively serious but with an inherently sound constitution recovery can be had through rest and convalescence. Kind: related to the head or chest regions.

Waiting for someone: The one who comes is friendly and will bring joy.

Looking for someone: The image is one of great distance. The search will take a lot of time. You should go in a northwesterly direction to conduct your search.

Lost article: You will find it, but you must be willing to spend some time. You should go in a northwesterly direction or to the northwest corner of something to conduct your search.

Travel: Propitious.

Lawsuit and disputes: If your case is reasonable you will win, but if you argue irrationally and unreasonably, the outcome will be very bad.

Employment: Be careful and diligent; going step by step you will reach your objective or expectation. Your superior may possibly promote you in rank or position; but you must be cautious.

Examination: High score, but you must not be lazy, lax, or idle.

New business, change of occupation or specialization, and moving: It is best to maintain your present status, situation, or position. However, new business ventures are auspicious.

Weather: Clear.

H E X A G R A M   2

K'UN

kun

The receptive

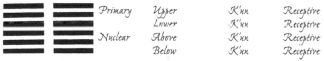

Primary	Upper	K'un	Receptive
	Lower	K'un	Receptive
Nuclear	Above	K'un	Receptive
	Below	K'un	Receptive

The *K'un* hexagram symbolizes the earth and represents the idea of yielding, gentleness, submissiveness, and obedience. It is the dark and maternal.

K'un is the opposite of the preceding *Ch'ien* hexagram; the six lines are all *yin*, or broken. The *yang* force represents giving, a strong or tough character or disposition, and positive movement or progress, while the *yin* represents receiving, compliancy, negativeness, and passivity. Therefore, when you arrive at this hexagram, you should be yielding like a mare, doing your duty or fulfilling your role and listening to and following the advice of your elders. In this way, through steadfastness, your prospects will open up in the near future.

THE FORTUNE

Do not be rash or reckless and do not act in a radical, heedless manner. Maintain the present. Carefully and attentively do your duty. Follow the ideas and thoughts of the capable and the wise and you will be benefited.

Wish: Cannot be accomplished right away. But do not be impatient and nervous. Success is possible through proceeding step by step in an orderly fashion and through persistence.

Marriage: A meek, obedient, and yielding bride.

Love: Success possible, but you must not be selfish or disregard the feelings of the other. Overly impatient or impetuous behavior will end in failure.

Family: Safe, sound, and happy.

Children: Many children, compatible and happy; girls will outnumber boys. Pregnancy: girl.

Capital loan: The loan cannot be settled at once. You will realize your goal if you patiently persist.

Business: You should not take action; best to wait for a better opportunity.

Stock market: Prices are low; buy now and wait for an opportunity to sell.

Life span: Physically weak, but if you take care of yourself you can have a long life.

Sickness: Afflictions of the abdominal region; not serious, but if neglected they will become chronic.

Waiting for someone: This person will not appear at once, but maybe a few days later.

Looking for someone: Nearby, look to the southwest.

Lost article: If it is not inside the house, it is lost. Look in the southwest.

Travel: It is best not to go on a trip for a while.

Lawsuit and disputes: Not advantageous; best to compromise.

Employment: Employment will not be found quickly; you must wait for the right time.

Examination: Average score.

New business, change of occupation or specialization, and moving: It is not the right time; you should wait for the correct moment.

Weather: Continually cloudy or rainy.

HEXAGRAM 3

CHUN

zhun

Difficulty at the beginning

Primary	Upper	K'an	Abysmal
	Lower	Chen	Arousing
Nuclear	Above	Ken	Keeping still
	Below	K'un	Receptive

Chun symbolizes the beginning of all things. Like young buds weak and unable to withstand severe winds and rain, the situation at the inception is one filled with hardships, difficulties, and obstacles. Endure the present difficulties, making efforts in silence. Your troubles will naturally dissipate and a chance for favorable change will come your way.

THE FORTUNE

If you start a business you will encounter many hazards and difficulties. Do not act rashly or blindly. You must have the fortitude to struggle with determination and dedication. If you make an all-out effort your troubles will gradually be resolved and success reached.

Wish: Very difficult to be realized. Forbearance and perseverance are needed to bring about success.

Marriage: Difficult. But for late marriages there is hope.

Love: Many obstacles and troubles for those in love. You must be patient and faithful.

Family: Ups and downs, unstable, difficulties. If harmony can be reached then prosperity and joy can be attained.

Children: Many children. At first it is difficult to avoid hardships, but later there will be a turn for the better. Pregnancy: boy.

Capital loan: Objective not easily obtained. The only chance is to work patiently, diligently pressing the matter forward.

Business: Will not go according to expectations. Do not become excited, impatient, or impulsive. Wait for the opportune moment.

Stock market: Continued slump.

Life span: Physically weak while young but with proper care of the body, strength will come after maturity.

Sickness: Serious and long-term, but hope lies in a gradual cure. Afflictions of the ear, nose, heart, and kidneys, and neurosis.

Waiting for someone: Will not appear soon; will appear only after the passage of a considerable period of time.

Looking for someone: The one you look for is experiencing hardships. It is not clear in which direction he has gone or where he is.

Lost article: It is still inside your home, room, office—indoors. But if you are separated from the article for too long a time you will not find it, and it will easily fall into someone else's hands and never return. Search in the east or north.

Travel: Trouble and delays in the course of the journey. Better stay at home.

Lawsuit and disputes: Time-consuming and tedious. Disadvantage or adversity will come from quarreling or irrational acts.

Employment: For the time being very difficult.

Examinations: Substandard score.

New business, change of occupation or specialization, and moving: Many obstacles; realization difficult. Better to wait for a more opportune moment before acting.

Weather: Cloudy, rainy, perhaps even thunder; later clearing.

H E X A G R A M 4

MENG

meng

Youthful folly

	Primary	Upper	Ken	Keeping still
		Lower	K'an	Abysmal
	Nuclear	Above	K'un	Receptive
		Below	Chen	Arousing

Meng symbolizes the inexperienced youth with unconfirmed views and undeveloped wisdom or intellect. These youths can, however, acquire acumen, wisdom, and knowledge through instruction and guidance. Examining the shape of the hexagram, we find that the top half, the trigram *Ken*, stands for the mountains while the bottom half, the trigram *K'an*, stands for water. Water becomes fog or mist when vaporized, covering or concealing the mountain, obscuring it so its real shape or face cannot be distinguished. *Meng* therefore connotes ignorance, stupidity, vagueness, and even unconsciousness. Everything is in a thick fog, groping about, and not very well developed. You must strive hard and listen to and follow the instructions and guidance of the intelligent, wise, and virtuous. If you do so all will gradually turn for the better.

THE FORTUNE

Slow and desultory, many difficulties and hardships. Moreover the facts and principles involved are not clear. There is a lack of decisiveness and determination. Hesitation and uncertainty in handling affairs often lead to errors, mistakes, and mismanagement. You should follow or obey the instructions of your elders, receiving the instruction with humility and an open mind. With patience, self-respect, and self-discipline wait for a turn to the better. A bright future will then draw near.

Wish: Very difficult to attain your wish. Wait patiently for a favorable chance.

Marriage: The chance for success is uncertain. There is nothing to do for the moment but wait. The other party is in a faraway place.

Love: Not knowing how to handle the situation and a lack of decision will result in failure.

Family: Circumstances difficult; moreover, neither congenial nor harmonious. All must treat each other with sincerity to improve the situation.

Children: Many children; consequently complications and entanglements are many. Pay attention to the upbringing of the children and they will bring blessings in the future. Pregnancy: boy.

Capital loan: Success very difficult.

Business: Not smooth, troublesome. You must wait for a better moment.

Stock market: Price unstable; will rise later.

Life span: Sick and weak. There is the possibility of a short life. You must emphasize taking care of your health.

Sickness: Afflictions of the brain and lower abdominal regions; contagious diseases. Time-consuming and lengthy. Emphasize rest and convalescence and there is hope of recuperating.

Waiting for someone: Will arrive at the destination late, making you wait.

Looking for someone: That someone has been enticed, tempted, or led astray. The search will be time-consuming. Look from the east to the north.

Lost article: Misplaced or left under something; look from the east to the north.

Travel: Many obstacles and delays. The decision should be made with caution and deliberation.

Lawsuit and disputes: Adversity. Will be postponed and drag on without reaching any conclusion; not worth the effort.

Employment: Cannot at once be found. You must be patient and keep trying hard.

Examination: Poor score.

New business, change of occupation or specialization, and moving: Not the right time; better wait.

Weather: Cloudy and rainy.

HSU

xu

Waiting (Nourishment)

	Primary	Upper	K'an	Abysmal
		Lower	Ch'ien	Creative
	Nuclear	Above	Li	Clinging
		Below	Tui	Joyous

Hsu means to wait. The lower trigram is *Ch'ien*, representing robustness, activeness, and aggressiveness. The upper trigram is *K'an* representing danger and thereby blocking the activity, liveliness, and function of *Ch'ien*. This hexagram implies that one should avoid danger caused by extreme radicalism and overanxious forward movement, waiting patiently with self-respect and self-discipline for a better and more opportune moment to arrive before pushing forward. The overall meaning is to wait or bide one's time.

THE FORTUNE

Observe the proper way and be determined and dedicated. Do not be rash, heedless, or overly extreme in actions. Wait for the opportune moment and your luck will gradually change. You will then in the end realize your expectations and aspirations. If you covet petty advantage or benefit that appears before you, you are bound to suffer failure.

Wish: Cannot be realized at once. Success will come only if you continue to strive with perseverance.

Marriage: Delays, obstacles, and vexation. Much effort but all in vain. The only chance for success is through patient perseverance and constant striving.

Love: Impulsiveness will lead to failure. Patient contact and honesty while waiting will lead to success.

Family: For the time being petty complications and bother. You must plan with decision and determination for the prosperity of the family.

Children: Children will come late. Pregnancy: boy.

Capital loan: For the moment you will face difficulties. You must spend a considerable amount of time in making contacts and in negotiations to bring about a good result.

Business: Do not covet immediate realization of petty gains. Be calm and steady, waiting for the right chance to act—otherwise the result will be failure.

Stock market: Sluggish for a while but will rise later.

Life span: When young, difficult to avoid sickness. Good health will come later.

Sickness: Long and protracted. With rest and convalescence you will recover. Digestive ailments or diseases afflicting the stomach, bowels, brain, or blood.

Waiting for someone: Will come late. You must wait patiently.

Looking for someone: It will take a long time to find this person but all will be well during this period. Look to either the north or the northwest.

Lost article: A long time will be spent before the article is found. Look to the north or the northwest.

Travel: For the moment, obstacles. There will be delay before you can begin.

Lawsuit and disputes: Not favorable. Better to compromise or drop it entirely.

Employment: You will not find work for the moment. Wait and a good job will come.

Examination: Will not go as expected. Study or practice harder.

New business, change of occupation or specialization, and moving: Not the right time. Wait for a better moment.

Weather: Cloudy and later rain.

SUNG

song

Conflict

	Primary	Upper	Chien	Creative
		Lower	K'an	Abysmal
	Nuclear	Above	Sun	Gentle
		Below	Li	Changing

Sung has the meaning of litigation, to bring something to court, and to dispute. The upper trigram is *Ch'ien*, representing the robustness of the *yang*, and implies advancement and upward movement. The lower trigram is *K'an*, which symbolizes water. Water flows downward. The two trigrams are thus opposed to each other. Moreover, *Ch'ien* rules or orders the lower through power while *K'an* resists the higher through devious means. Therefore this hexagram suggests that things are complicated, full of disputes, obstacles, and conflict. It is not an auspicious hexagram.

THE FORTUNE

Nothing will go according to expectations or desires. Everything is full of trouble, bother, complications, and obstacles. It is not advantageous to advance forward or to proceed. It is better to retreat and maintain a position, waiting for your fortune to change.

Wish: Cannot be achieved.

Marriage: Not advantageous or propitious. Moreover, it will not succeed.

Love: The other side is not sincere enough. It will end in failure.

Family: Family members are on bad terms; mutual ties must be strengthened.

Children: A conflict of ideas and opinions exists between father and son. Pregnancy: boy.

Capital loan: Very difficult.

Business: Improper handling, resulting in a loss.

Stock market: Rising and falling—unstable.

Life span: Many illnesses and a short life. You must be very careful about taking care of your health.

Sickness: Serious, with many changes and complications. Afflictions of the brain, lungs, kidneys, and blood system.

Waiting for someone: Will not come.

Looking for someone: This person has gone off because of an argument, dispute, or fight. Look in the north and northwest.

Lost article: It has already fallen into someone else's hands. It will not be easy to get it back.

Travel: Many hindrances along the way; you will not reach your destination. It is better to quit than to try to go all the way.

Lawsuit and disputes: Not favorable. It is best to compromise.

Employment: You will not succeed in finding a job.

Examination: Poor score.

New business, change of occupation or specialization, and moving: Adversity. Cannot succeed, so do not proceed.

Weather: Uncertain and changeable, cloudy and rainy.

HEXAGRAM 7

SHIH

shi

The army

Primary	*Upper*	*K'un*	*Receptive*
	Lower	*K'an*	*Abysmal*
Nuclear	*Above*	*K'un*	*Receptive*
	Below	*Chen*	*Arousing*

Shih symbolizes armies and multitudes and incorporates the idea of fighting or waging war. The second line from the bottom is a solid, *yang* line and symbolizes a great general commanding or leading the other five *yin* lines. The upper trigram is *K'un*, the earth; the bottom trigram is *K'an*, which symbolizes water. When water is on the earth it dampens and enriches a myriad of things, but in this hexagram the proper position is turned around. The earth sits atop the water. The two cannot come together in harmony. In divination, this hexagram means contention, quarrels, complications, and chaos. The only way to achieve a turn for the better is to earnestly keep to the true and correct path.

THE FORTUNE

Change, movement, and undulations. The waves are great and hardships many. Do not flaunt petty schemes and devious means. Plan for yourself, uphold the correct path, and handle affairs with decision, determination, and perseverance and you will be able to overcome all difficulties, realizing distinction, rank, profit, or advantage.

Wish: A great variety of difficulties. It is hard for you to realize your wish. The only hope is to be patient and stick with it, working hard.

Marriage: Not a happy match, many problems, shortcomings and blemishes will appear.

Love: The other party is unstable and frivolous. The love is not shared mutually. Many complications will arise.

Family: It appears that family members do not get along. There should be more understanding and sincerity between them.

Children: Daughters more than sons. Pregnancy: boy.

Capital loan: It will not be granted right away. There is hope if you remain patient and persist in seeing the matter through.

Business: Obstacles. Profit or advantage will be yours if you wait until you have more confidence and the situation is more to your favor before acting with decision.

Stock market: Uncertain, unstable situation. There is a possibility the market will rise.

Life span: Your health is questionable. You must take very good care of yourself.

Sickness: Serious but not fatal. Malignant tumors, diseases of the heart and abdomen.

Waiting for someone: Will not come.

Looking for someone: This person has gone away because of a falling out or a difference of opinion. Look to the southwest or to the north.

Lost article: It has already been appropriated by a woman. It will be difficult to get the article back.

Travel: There is a possibility of some natural calamity occurring. Best not to go on a trip.

Lawsuit and disputes: Complications and difficulties. You can succeed with firm and strong tactics.

Employment: No hope.

Examination: Poor score.

New business, change of occupation or specialization, and moving: Adversity. Best not to move.

Weather: Changeable weather. Cloudy, later clearing—but not for sure.

Pí

bi

Holding together (Union)

	Primary	Upper	K'an	Abysmal
		Lower	K'un	Receptive
	Nuclear	Above	Ken	Keeping Still
		Below	K'un	Receptive

Pi symbolizes closeness or intimacy. The fifth line from the bottom, the controlling line or ruler's line, is solid. This *yang* line asserts itself over all the other *yin* (broken) lines. The upper trigram *K'an* symbolizes water and the bottom trigram *K'un* symbolizes the earth. When water is poured over the earth, it seeps into the ground and becomes one with the dirt and clay, blending and coming together. It is the auspicious sign of heaven loving and cherishing the people, when above and below are in harmony, close together, and helping each other. In divination, it means that contact with others will go well and all will be done smoothly.

THE FORTUNE

Peaceful, safe, propitious. You should mix with people and become close to others. But if you act shamelessly or unreasonably you will ruin this good fortune. It would be auspicious for you to unite or cooperate with others in doing something. The good fortune also includes the support or confidence of the public and of development or progress in affairs.

Wish: You will succeed with the help of someone else.

Marriage: Success and happiness.

Love: Auspicious. Both sides love each other. Nevertheless, women must beware of rivals. "The early bird gets the worm."

Family: Everyone is on good terms. Family fortunes are flourishing.

Children: Well-behaved, helpful. Loyal. Pregnancy: boy.

Capital loan: Definite success.

Business: Will go as hoped and profits will be realized. Greed will cause misfortune to strike later.

Stock market: Fluctuations with a possibility of prices going down.

Life span: Healthy, long life.

Sickness: Recovery or cure in the not distant future. Diseases of the blood system.

Waiting for someone: Will come, bringing happiness.

Looking for someone: Do not worry. He will be found soon or will return on his own initiative.

Lost article: Will be found. Search to the north or southwest, in low-lying places, or near water.

Travel: Safe and sound journey. Moreover you will gain something from it.

Lawsuit and disputes: Compromise is not only easy but it will bring benefit. To contest obstinately will lead to adversity.

Employment: Promotion or a good position or job will be found.

Examination: Good score.

New business, change of occupation or specialization, and moving: Propitious.

Weather: Clear, later cloudy. Rain is a possibility.

HEXAGRAM 9

HSIAO CH'U

xiao chu

The taming power of the small

Primary	Upper	Sun	Gentle
	Lower	Ch'ien	Receptive
Nuclear	Above	Li	Clinging
	Below	'Tui	Joyous

The image of this hexagram is the weather, when thick clouds have appeared but, as yet, no rain. The upper trigram is *Sun* and represents the wind and clouds. The bottom trigram is *Ch'ien*, or heaven. When wind and clouds dominate the heavens, the weather is depressing, as if it is about to rain but without actually raining. Looking at such a sky one feels nervous and impatient. Thus this hexagram implies that things will not go smoothly.

THE FORTUNE
Rough and full of obstacles. Things will not go as expected.

Do not be pessimistic, languid, or intemperate. Be patient and keep striving, for after the clouds scatter there will be sunshine and your luck will change.

Wish: Obstacles will prevent you from reaching your goal.

Marriage: Not well matched. Moreover, many obstacles stand in the way.

Love: Many obstacles; success will not come easily. Even if you succeed, the final curtain will close on a tragic scene.

Family: Husband and wife are fed up with each other for the moment, listless and indifferent. A depressed air has settled over the whole family. The only thing to do is wait for a while.

Children: Anxiety for your children will cause you toil and drudgery. Pregnancy: girl.

Capital loan: A woman will act as an impediment, hindering any outcome.

Business: Conditions not ripe for thriving business. Unknown stumbling blocks will prevent your transaction from being realized or consummated.

Stock market: Outlook gloomy.

Life span: Poor health, weak body, and the possibility of a short life. You must take good care of your health.

Sickness: Lengthy sickness, possibly becoming chronic. Venereal disease, diseases of the uterus, chest area, and abdomen.

Waiting for someone: Midway along the way something has prevented this person from coming.

Looking for someone: It appears that disharmony in the family has caused that person to leave. Sexual passion may also have some bearing on the situation. This person will not be found easily; but, on the other hand, he has not gone far. Search to the southeast or northwest.

Lost article: Not easily found. Perhaps lying under some object.

Travel: Many obstacles, time-consuming or delaying. You will not realize the purpose of your travel. It is better not to make the trip.

Lawsuit and disputes: Lengthy and drawn out; many difficulties will arise.

Employment: For the moment, no hope.

Examination: Poor score.

New business, change of occupation or specialization, and moving: Will not go as hoped or expected. Wait for a better chance.

Weather: Heavy clouds but no rain.

LÜ

lü

Treading (Conduct)

Primary	*Upper*	*Ch'ien*	*Creative*
	Lower	*Tui*	*Joyous*
Nuclear	*Above*	*Sun*	*Gentle*
	Below	*Li*	*Clinging*

Lü symbolizes walking behind the tail of a tiger but not being in any danger. The upper trigram is *Ch'ien* and the lower one is *Tui*. The hexagram conjures up the picture of the robust and strong male *Ch'ien* walking in front with the delicate and weak female *Tui* following. It is hard for her not to fall behind. *Lü* also means propriety or courtesy. The trigram *Tui* with its virtue of gentle meekness receives the strength and robustness of the *Ch'ien*. For this reason, though there is danger in walking behind the tail of a tiger, the tiger will not bite and the walk will be safe.

The meaning of the hexagram is though there are difficulties and obstacles, a gentle, yielding, and amiable attitude will bring you through safe and sound.

THE FORTUNE

Trouble and danger all around. But if you bide your time patiently, with humility and meekness, good fortune will be yours. Do not take the initiative or offensive. Maintain your position.

Wish: Very difficult to be realized.

Marriage: Although both parties are well suited for each other, many stumbling blocks will appear to make culmination of the marriage difficult. If you persevere with politeness and the proper decorum you might succeed.

Love: The path is strewn with hardships, but if you keep the sincere heart of your initial affection and continue to strive hard there is hope for success.

Family: Hardships and difficulties at first. If you maintain an attitude of patience, humility, and gentleness, good fortune and blessings will be yours in middle age.

Children: Difficulty in rearing your children, but later your luck will change. Pregnancy: girl.

Capital loan: Very difficult to be realized.

Business: Obstacles and hardship.

Stock market: Prices will drop. It is best to hold your position, for the market will later recover.

Life span: Weak when young. But through careful care of your health, you may have a long life.

Sickness: Serious, but with convalescence you may recover your health. Brain or lung diseases.

Waiting for someone: Will come but will be late.

Looking for someone: In danger at the moment. If not saved or found in time, there is danger of harm. Search in the northwest.

Lost article: Covered up, lying underneath something. Search to the northwest.

Travel: Hardships and danger; best to reconsider.

Lawsuit and disputes: Unpropitious; best to seek a compromise.

Employment: For the moment not to be found. Wait patiently for a better opportunity.

Examination: Just passing.

New business, change of occupation or specialization, and moving: Many obstacles. Realization difficult.

Weather: Cloudy, wind in the afternoon.

T'AI

tai

Peace

	Primary	Upper	K'un	Receptive
		Lower	Ch'ien	Creative
	Nuclear	Above	Chen	Arousing
		Below	Tui	Joyous

T'ai symbolizes peace and harmony. The upper trigram is *Ch'ien* representing heaven and the lower one is *K'un* standing for earth. The *yin* force of *K'un* pushes downward while the *yang* force of *Ch'ien* pushes upward. This means that the forces of heaven and earth and *yin* and *yang* are equal, matched and fused—united together. All things as a result are growing and flourishing. In divining, this hexagram is very auspicious, indicating peace and fortune.

THE FORTUNE

Everything will go as expected or hoped; the future looks good. Business will flourish. There may even be an occasion for joy (such as a wedding). But you must not for this reason be arrogant, remiss, careless, or negligent.

Wish. Smoothly accomplished.

Marriage: Well suited for each other, compatible. Everything will go smoothly.

Love: Compatible and congenial.

Family: Harmonious relationships; the family fortunes will flourish.

Children: All well and enjoying good fortune. However, you must not be remiss in their education. Pregnancy: boy.

Capital loan: Will go smoothly.

Business: Smooth. Moreover you will reap a great profit.

Stock market: High now but will go down later.

Life span: Healthy, long life.

Sickness: Will recover or be cured soon. Diseases afflicting the head.

Waiting for someone: Will come bringing joy.

Looking for someone: Something to do with sex. Staying in the house of a friend or relative. You will find this person soon. Look in the southwest or northwest.

Lost article: Mistakenly placed into something. You will find it soon.

Travel: Safe and sound.

Lawsuit and disputes: You will gain advantage or benefit if you compromise. Adversity will come from stubbornly carrying on the dispute.

Employment: You will encounter no difficulties.

Examination: Good scores, but you must be cautious.

New business, change of occupation or specialization, and moving: You may plan to proceed. Success will be yours.

Weather: Fine weather.

HEXAGRAM 12

P'I

pi

Standstill (Stagnation)

Primary	Upper	Ch'ien	Creative
	Lower	K'un	Receptive
Nuclear	Above	Sun	Gentle
	Below	Ken	Keeping Still

P'i symbolizes obstruction or stagnation. It is the opposite of the preceding hexagram. The upper trigram is *Ch'ien*, or heaven, and its robust *yang* force is elevated upward. The lower trigram is *K'un*, or earth, and its *yin* force is depressed downward. The forces of heaven and earth and *yin* and *yang* are blocked and separated. There is no free flow between them. In divining, this hexagram stands for toil and hardship. Moreover, you will not get the help of others.

In politics it means there is no meeting of minds between the government and the people. The feeling of the people is not reflected in the government and government policies do not have the support of the people.

THE FORTUNE
Unlucky. Things will not go as hoped. Instead, you will experience toil and hardship. Petty people or evil men may even inflict injury, harm, and loss on you. You may even experience the pain of parting or separation. There is a natural principle of rise and fall and of rotation in the world, so your luck may change if you remain with it, striving patiently with courage. It is best to maintain your present circumstances.

Wish: Very difficult.

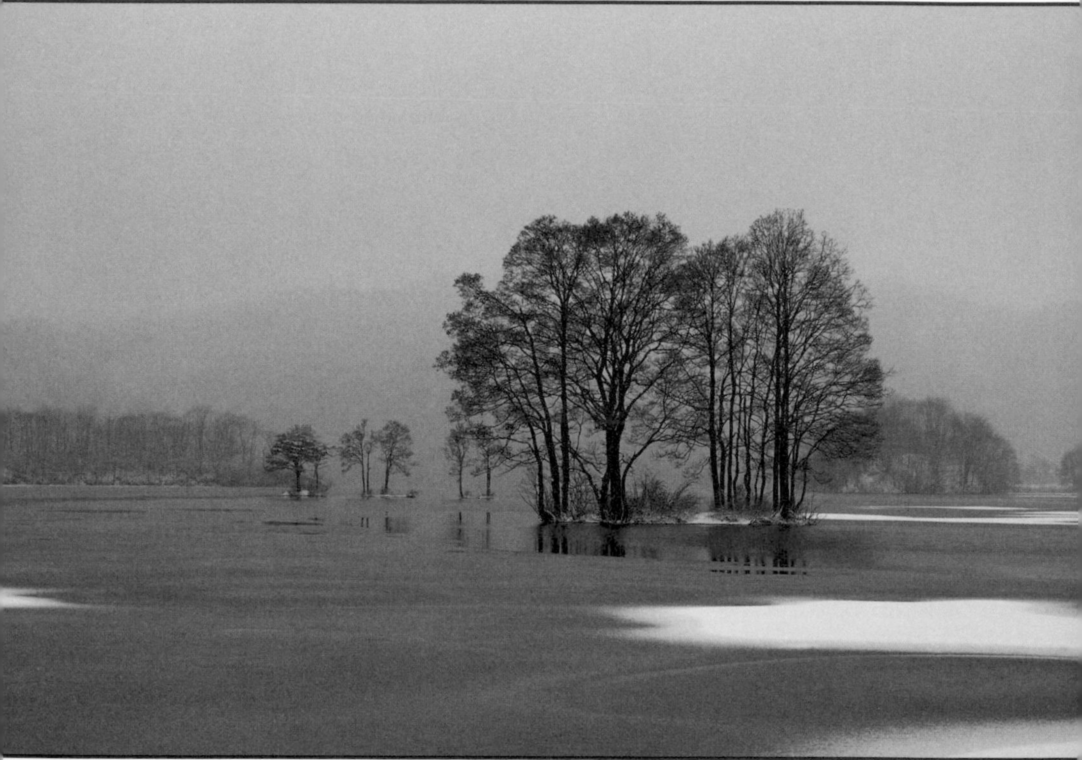

Marriage: The two are neither suited for each other nor compatible. Moreover, it appears the two may part.

Love: The other party does not feel the same way.

Family: Family members are on bad terms with each other. There is also the possibility of hard times.

Children: Few children if any. There may be bad feelings between parents and children. Pregnancy: girl.

Capital loan: Unsuccessful. Economic circulation sluggish.

Business: Deficit or losses.

Stock market: Prices low.

Life span: Weak, ill health—a short life.

Sickness: Serious. There is a chance you will not regain your health. Diseases of the respiratory organs and brain, cancer.

Waiting for someone: In vain.

Looking for someone: This person has gone away because of ill feeling or being jilted. It is not clear where this person has gone.

Lost article: It has already fallen into someone else's hands. You will not get it back.

Travel: Trouble and obstacles. There is no way to reach your destination. Better cancel travel plans.

Lawsuit and disputes: Defeat.

Employment: No hope.

Examination: Bad score.

New business, change of occupation or specialization, and moving: Not the right time, difficult to be realized. Safest thing to do is drop all such plans.

Weather: Bad.

T'UNG JEN

tong ren

Fellowship with men

	Primary	Upper	Ch'ien	Receptive
		Lower	Li	Clinging
	Nuclear	Above	Ch'ien	Receptive
		Below	Sun	Gentle

T'ung Jen symbolizes like-mindedness, concert or harmony, fellowship and universal brotherhood. It means that one can get along with others—cooperation and harmony in efforts. It also means comrade, friend, colleague, or companion. The upper trigram is *Ch'ien*, or heaven, while the lower is *Li*, or fire. Both have the characteristic of upward motion. Lines two, three, and four from the bottom form the nuclear trigram *Sun*, which represents the wind. Aided by wind, the flames of the fire will violently leap upward, coming close to the heaven above and reflecting brilliance. It symbolizes relationships with others and that success will come with the help of or in cooperation with others.

THE FORTUNE

Safe and sound, propitious. Things will go as you hope. All business conducted in concert with others will succeed. You should expand interpersonal relationships, make more friends. When you acquire harmony with others, good fortune will open up for you. You must not act selfishly, disregarding the opinions of others, or be biased, thus damaging a fair or just position. Avoid quarrels and disputes with others.

Wish: Can be realized. You will benefit more if you act with the aid of others than alone.

Marriage: Compatible and well suited for each other.

Love: Each feels the same for the other. Success will come naturally.

Family: Compatible; family fortunes flourishing.

Children: Many children, harmonious relationships. Pregnancy: boy.

Capital loan: Success.

Business: Great profit, especially if the business is a cooperative venture with others.

Stock market: Prices will rise.

Life span: Healthy and long life.

Sickness: Will be cured or recover soon. Infections of the stomach and intestines.

Waiting for someone: Will come, bringing joy.

Looking for someone: Will return soon or will send a message.

Lost article: You will find it soon.

Travel: Safe and sound journey. Great fun.

Lawsuit and disputes: Best to compromise. Stubborn insistence on seeing the dispute through will put you at a disadvantage.

Employment: You will find work quickly.

Examination: Good score.

New business, change of occupation or specialization, and moving: Propitious.

Weather: Clear.

TA YU

da you

Possession in great measure

	Primary	Upper	Li	Clinging
		Lower	Chien	Creative
	Nuclear	Above	Tui	Joyous
		Below	Chien	Creative

Ta Yu symbolizes great abundance, wealth, and possession. The upper trigram is *Li*, which symbolizes the sun. The lower trigram is *Ch'ien*, or heaven. The sun is high in the sky, shining down on all things. The *Li* trigram also represents the summer season when all things are flourishing. The lower trigram represents autumn when all things have reached maturity and the time for the harvest has arrived, implying abundance and wealth. In divining, it means that you are in the midst of a period of extreme good fortune. But after the zenith, decline will come. Therefore, you must be cautious, prudent, and careful. You must not be haughty and overbearing.

THE FORTUNE

You are enjoying good fortune and public respect. Great profit or benefit will be yours. But in all things you must be prudent and cautious in order to maintain your good fortune. Otherwise, it will be difficult to avoid satiation, then deficiency and a downward trend.

Wish: Achieved smoothly.

Marriage: Well matched. There is a possibility you will marry wealth.

Love: Success.

Family: Enjoying good fortune and prosperity. To be careless, remiss, or arrogant and self-satisfied will bring about a reversal of the flourishing family fortunes.

Children: They have promise and ability. However, you cannot be remiss in their education and rearing. Pregnancy: girl.

Capital loan: No difficulties.

Business: You can reap great profits.

Stock market: Prices at a peak. Beware, for prices may begin to drop.

Life span: You are by nature healthy. Long life.

Sickness: Rapid recovery. High fevers, afflictions of the lungs.

Waiting for someone: Will arrive bearing good tidings.

Looking for someone: Appears to be far away. Money or sex is involved. You must search rapidly. Procrastination will cause failure. Look in the south or northwest.

Lost article: Can be found. Search in the south or northwest—high places.

Travel: Propitious.

Lawsuit and disputes: Satisfactory outcome.

Employment: Propitious. A good job with a degree of position or prestige will be yours.

Examination: Excellent score. But you must continue to work hard.

New business, change of occupation or specialization, and moving: Propitious.

Weather: Fine, clear.

CH'IEN

qian

Modesty

	Primary	Upper	*K'un*	*Receptive*
		Lower	*Ken*	*Keeping Still*
	Nuclear	Above	*Chen*	*Arousing*
		Below	*K'an*	*Abysmal*

Ch'ien means humility and modesty. The upper trigram is *K'un*, or earth. The lower trigram is *Ken*, representing mountains. Tall mountains bend and dwell below the great plain, symbolizing the virtue of modesty and humility. *Ch'ien* also means to give one's surplus to those who do not have enough. The idea is to transport the dirt of a high mountain to fill in a low-lying place. In divining, it means that prosperity and good fortune will come if you maintain humility and sincerity in actions.

THE FORTUNE

Safe and sound; everything will go as hoped. You will summon failure if you violate the path of humility and modesty. You must be humble.

Wish: Selfish, narrow-minded, and ungenerous conduct will bring failure. Treat others with sincerity when performing an action and accomplishment will be yours.

Marriage: Well matched. Smooth and good luck.

Love: Success.

Family: Satisfactory. The family fortunes will gradually develop.

Children: All gentle, obedient, loyal. Pregnancy: boy.

Capital loans: Negotiation possible for the money you need, but no hope for extra money.

Business: A low margin of profit on sales will add up if sales are many.

Stock market: For the moment sluggish, will rise later.

Life span: With rest and care you may have a healthy and long life.

Sickness: With patience you will recover gradually through convalescence. Diseases afflicting the abdomen or belly, low blood pressure.

Waiting for someone: Will come.

Looking for someone: Will return on his own initiative.

Lost article: You can find it. Underneath something in the northeast or southwest.

Travel: Safe and sound journey.

Lawsuit and disputes: Better to seek a compromise. To continue the battle stubbornly will bring you misfortune.

Employment: No problem.

Examination: Good score.

New business, change of occupation or specialization, and moving: You may proceed, but haste and impulsiveness will lead to misfortune.

Weather: Cloudy with possible clearing from time to time.

HEXAGRAM 16

YÜ

yü

Enthusiasm

Primary	Upper	Chen	Arousing
	Lower	K'un	Receptive
Nuclear	Above	K'an	Abysmal
	Below	Ken	Keeping Still

Yü means beforehand and connotes such ideas as premonition, to know beforehand, and preparation. The upper trigram is *Chen*, representing thunder, and the lower trigram is *K'un*, or earth. After the spring thunder appears on earth, the sun will shine down on all things. The trees, flowers, and grasses will be given life and they will sprout and grow. The appearance is happy and cheerful. For mankind too it is the time to prepare for new work, new actions. In divining, it means the coming of joy and cheer. But one must make careful preparations in advance and proceed with caution, never relaxing. In this way good fortune will be maintained; otherwise, calamity will strike.

THE FORTUNE

Everything will go as hoped. But you cannot relax and be idle or negligent. If you are, you will bring bad luck and bitterness upon yourself. At the same time you must discipline yourself in your private life and put your personal papers and documents of proof in order so as to protect yourself against some unexpected trouble or complication. Moreover, beware of robbers.

Wish: Proceed with caution, step by step, and you can accomplish what you want.

Marriage: A good match, preordained by heaven. Smooth union.

Love: Can succeed. If both sides act selfishly or in disregard for the feelings of the other, the result will be failure.

Family: Abundance and blessings from birth. Ruin will descend upon you if you are careless, idle, or lead a lazy, good-for-nothing life.

Children: Children love each other. Harmonious. Unlimited future. But you must pay heed to their upbringing. Negligence will bring about misfortune. Pregnancy: boy.

Capital loan: If you are cautious and prudent in handling the affair you will succeed.

Business: High prices mean profits for you.

Stock market: Prices high.

Life span: Healthy and long life. But if you dissipate yourself in pleasures you will encounter the opposite.

Sickness: Will recover, but you must take care in convalescing. Liver and abdominal disorders or related afflictions.

Waiting for someone: Will come.

Looking for someone: Intoxicated with pleasure. Look in the east or southwest.

Lost article: Lost or stolen. If you wait too long, you will not get the article back. Search in the east or southwest.

Travel: Propitious, but you must be careful while on the journey.

Lawsuit and disputes: Advantageous for you to seek a compromise. Adversity will come from stubbornly carrying on the case.

Employment: Can be found. If you already have a job, your boss will take a liking to you and give you a promotion.

Examination: Good score, but you must continue to work hard.

New business, change of occupation or specialization, and moving: Propitious.

Weather: Cloudy, later clearing.

SUI

sui

Following

Primary	Upper	Tui	Joyous
	Lower	Chen	Arousing
Nuclear	Above	Sun	Gentle
	Below	Ken	Keeping Still

Sui means to follow, to obey, to accord with, and to accompany. It implies yielding to the opinions or viewpoints of others, not insisting on one's own opinion. It also implies going along with the vicissitudes of fortune and the changes wrought by time. The upper trigram is *Tui*, representing young girls, while the lower trigram *Chen* stands for strong men. The hexagram implies that the strong man docilely and obediently follows the young girl. In divining, *Sui* symbolizes the strong submitting to the weak, thereby gaining the willing compliance of the multitude and success in affairs.

THE FORTUNE

Respect the opinions of others and use the assistance provided by others—then the undertaking will be a success and both fame and fortune will be yours.

Wish: You will succeed after a delay of some time if you gain the assistance of others.

Marriage: Success is a possibility. The appearance is of a young woman marrying an older man.

Love: Success. But if you merely satisfy sensual desires there is a possibility of feelings being hurt and the relationship breaking up.

Family: Born into a wealthy and lucky family. There is a possibility for boys to be foster sons (adopted) and for the girls alone to be responsible for the livelihood of the whole family.

Children: Parents and children are in harmony. Pregnancy: girl.

Capital loan: Although there will be a delay, sooner or later a friend will lend his assistance and you will succeed.

Business: Smooth. However you cannot expand at once. You must wait for the opportune moment.

Stock market: High now but will slowly fall.

Life span: Healthy and long life. But you must not be careless and abuse your body.

Sickness: The period of sickness will be protracted, but recovery is possible. Venereal disease or kidney ailments.

Waiting for someone: Will come, but will be late.

Looking for someone: Will be found soon. The person has gone away because of something to do with sex.

Lost article: It is close by and you will find it. Search to the east or west.

Travel: Better not go on the trip alone. Best to go with a companion.

Lawsuit and disputes: Adversity—perhaps even imprisonment. Best to seek a compromise.

Employment: If an elder or superior takes an interest, you will succeed.

Examination: Good score.

New business, change of occupation or specialization, and moving: Auspicious, but you must make sufficient plans and preparations.

Weather: Heavy rain and thunder.

HEXAGRAM 18

KU

gu

Work on that which has been spoiled (Decay)

Primary	Upper	Ken	Keeping Still
	Lower	Sun	Gentle
Nuclear	Above	Chen	Arousing
	Below	Tui	Joyous

Ku symbolizes the food on a plate which has rotted and become the home of worms. It implies chaos, corruption, ruin, delusion, refuse, and flaws. The upper trigram *Ken* represents the mountains while the lower *Sun* stands for the wind. The wind is below the mountain—being blocked by the mountain, it cannot move and flow. If the air cannot flow and circulate, things will begin to spoil and become wormy. In divining, it means that the situation around you is extremely confused and complicated. You must work to set things in order or maintain order—otherwise you will meet defeat. The removal of the decay can lead to success in reversing your fortunes.

THE FORTUNE

Everything is stopped and stagnant; many kinds of trouble and predicaments are present. At the same time, you must worry about your family. Your household affairs may also be in confusion and disarray. There may also be illicit love entanglements and sickness.

Wish: Not successful. Change your course and try again.

Marriage: Not destined for each other, ill-suited, and many problems. Better abandon this match.

Love: Already intimate but much trouble and distress. Best to sever relations at once.

Family: Family affairs in chaos, many vexations. You must put your household affairs back into order with determination or face the possibility that the whole family may be ruined and break up.

Children: Your children are not of sound moral character. As they create trouble all about, worrying about them will cause you great distress. You must be very strict in teaching and guiding them; otherwise the outcome will be unthinkable. Pregnancy: boy.

Capital loans: Unsuccessful.

Business: It appears that goods are accumulated and stored up but cannot be sold.

Stock market: Prices at a low ebb.

Life span: Sick and weak—even the possibility of a short life. You must pay attention to caring for your health.

Sickness: Serious, may even require surgery or other special treatment. Diseases afflicting the abdominal or stomach region.

Waiting for someone: Something has come up along the way and the person will not show.

Looking for someone: This person has left because of family incompatibility or improper behavior. Look to the northeast or southeast.

Lost article: Underneath something or in the bottom of a box. Search in the southeast or northeast.

Travel: Trouble along the way. Best to drop travel plans.

Lawsuit and disputes: Time-consuming, protracted. Not easily resolved. Better change tactics or course of action to gain an advantageous conclusion.

Employment: For the time being you will not find any.

Examination: Very bad score.

New business, change of occupation or specialization, and moving: Propitious, but you must select a new course of action.

Weather: Cloudy and windy.

H E X A G R A M   1 9

LIN

lin

Approach

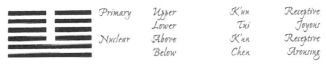

Primary	Upper	K'un	Receptive
	Lower	Tui	Joyous
Nuclear	Above	K'un	Receptive
	Below	Chen	Arousing

Lin means to expand, increase and advance. The bottom two lines of the hexagram are *yang* lines and mean that the *yang* force is on the rise, expanding, while the *yin* force is gradually retreating or receding. This hexagram also has the meaning of mutual aid or the mutual entrusting of expectations. In divining, it means that if you handle affairs in a yielding or cooperative manner, not using force, and treat others according to the correct rules of conduct, much good fortune will be yours.

THE FORTUNE
You will enjoy good fortune and everything will go as you hope. However, in order to maintain your good fortune you must be humble, not arrogant or haughty; and you must treat others gently and warmly.

Wish: Will be realized.

Marriage: Well suited for each other.

Love: Success is a possibility—but it can be hot and cold. You must remain calm and collected.

Family: Prosperous and lucky.

Children: Obedient, gentle, and loyal. However, you must not spoil them as a result. Pregnancy: girl.

Capital loans: Can be realized.

Business: Easy and smooth realization of profits.

Stock market: Booming; prices will go up.

Life span: Naturally healthy. You will lead a long life if you take care of your body.

Sickness: You will recover. Diseases afflicting the stomach, bowels, and urinary system; venereal disease.

Waiting for someone: Will come bringing joy and laughter.

Looking for someone: You will find this person soon or he will return on his own. Look to the west or southwest.

Lost article: You will find it. Look to the west or southwest.

Travel: Propitious.

Lawsuit and disputes: Beneficial for you to seek a compromise. Adversity will come by obstinately pushing on with the case.

Employment: You can find a job.

Examination: Good score.

New business, change of occupation or specialization, and moving: Auspicious, you may proceed.

Weather: Cloudy, later clearing.

HEXAGRAM 20

KUAN

guan

Contemplation (View)

Primary	Upper	Sun	Gentle
	Lower	K'un	Receptive
Nuclear	Above	Ken	Keeping Still
	Below	K'un	Receptive

Kuan means observation, inspection, contemplation, reflection, and self-examination. The upper trigram is *Sun* (wind) and the lower one is *K'un* (earth). The hexagram symbolizes a great wind blowing onto the earth. Therefore, it is a time for movement—shaking and trembling—and for cautious advancement. In divining, it suggests the calm and detached maintenance of the present position. Improvement can be had through reflection, contemplation, and self-examination.

THE FORTUNE

Beginning of the decline. You should reflect and examine yourself and treat others with sincerity in order to insure peace, tranquility, and your good fortune. If you are able to get the backing or support of your elders or superiors, there is the possibility of advancement.

Wish: It appears very hopeful on the surface, but in reality realization is very difficult.

Marriage: Many difficulties. There is no hope for success.

Love: Frequent quarrels. No hope for success.

Family: The family fortunes are going downhill. If you conduct yourself with the utmost sincerity in treating others and in handling affairs, plus working hard, you might be able to maintain the family's peace and prosperity.

Children: Many worries and much distress. If you work hard at bringing them up, then you will be able to see their success and fortune. Pregnancy: girl.

Capital loans: Success is difficult.

Business: Not smooth. But if you do not act impulsively and rashly and instead proceed carefully and in logical order, you will reap a profit.

Stock market: Prices oscillating, unstable. Will decline later.

Life span: Often ill. Take care of yourself and you will lead a long life.

Sickness: Many changes in the condition of the sickness. Whether you will be able to recover depends on convalescence and on applying the correct treatment. Diseases afflicting the organs of the respiratory system, the abdominal region, and the nervous system.

Waiting for someone: Trouble or accident along the way; he will not come. Even if he should come, he would cause disappointment.

Looking for someone: Drifting about in an uncertain direction. Look to the southeast or the southwest.

Lost article: It has already fallen into someone else's hands. Not easily recoverable.

Travel: Sightseeing trip suitable.

Lawsuit and disputes: A lot of work in vain. Best to compromise.

Employment: Very difficult at the present. Wait for a better moment.

Examination: Poor score.

New business, change of occupation or specialization, and moving: Not the right time.

Weather: Strong winds and unstable weather.

HEXAGRAM 21

SHIH HO

shi he

Biting through

	Primary	Upper	Li	Clinging
		Lower	Chen	Arousing
	Nuclear	Above	K'an	Abysmal
		Below	Ken	Keeping Still

Shih Ho has the meaning of the lips coming together again after biting or chewing something. The top and bottom *yang* lines represent the lips. *Yin* lines two, three, and five are the teeth. Line four, the *yang* line, is squeezed in between as though it were something being bitten or chewed. After the thing has been bitten the lips come together again. In divining, it means that obstacles stand in the way but you can reach your objective if the obstruction is removed or overcome—destroyed like chewing something into bits.

THE FORTUNE

Things will not go as you hope—many difficulties. You must take positive action. Passivity will mean failure along the way. If you go forward with courage, you can reach your destination without a doubt. There is the possibility that you will quarrel or get into a dispute with someone. The best thing to do is to handle the matter personally. Do not rely on others. There is also the possibility that someone may speak ill of you or that you will be harmed in some way because of a woman.

Wish: Obstacles make realization difficult. Realization might be possible if you attempt to overcome difficulties with a spirit of positive energy.

Marriage: At first there will be many obstacles and differences of opinion. But gradually your opinions will become of one accord. Success will depend on the extent to which you are positive in action.

Love: A person of the opposite sex will create a stumbling block midway. If you keep striving, success will be yours.

Family: Husband and wife are not compatible. Hardship and bitterness. If both are tolerant and yielding, things will get better in a while.

Children: The children are all strong-willed and willful. They do not listen to their parents, even resisting or going against them. You must strictly instruct and guide them. Pregnancy: girl.

Capital loans: Obstacles make realization difficult.

Business: Many obstacles. It will not go as hoped. Positive action will overcome the difficulties and you will reap a profit.

Stock market: Active market. Prices rising.

Life span: Many health problems. You must make a determined effort to discipline yourself, thereby ensuring your health.

Sickness: Serious. You must decide to undergo an operation or some other kind of special medical treatment in order to recover. Malignant diseases.

Waiting for someone: This person will not come. The best thing to do is to go look for this person.

Looking for someone: This person has gone away because of some dispute or involvement in a serious matter. He is in mortal danger. The best thing to do is ask the authorities to search.

Lost article. It has already fallen into someone else's hands and cannot be recovered.

Travel: It will be hard to avoid a mishap en route, but in the end you will reach your destination safely.

Lawsuit and disputes: A defiant, strong attitude will bring you victory.

Examination: Encountering difficult problems, you will not pass.

Employment: Difficult. Success will come only if you seek employment positively.

New business, change of occupation or specialization, and moving: Many obstacles. Proceed with vigor and you will succeed.

Weather: After strong rains and wind the weather will clear.

HEXAGRAM 22

PI

bi

Grace

Primary	*Upper*	Ken	*Keeping Still*
	Lower	Li	*Clinging*
Nuclear	*Above*	Chen	*Arousing*
	Below	Kan	*Abysmal*

Pi means to adorn, beautiful colors, beautiful appearances, elegance, to decorate, and decorations and ornaments. *Ken*, the upper diagram, stands for mountains. The lower trigram *Li* represents the sun. The hexagram thus symbolizes the sun setting behind the western mountains. All about there is the beautiful and exhilarating scene of a sunset. In divining, it means the waning of a beautiful period. Beautiful on the surface, it will soon fade away. When the sun sets behind the mountains, the strength of its rays are limited, symbolizing that what one sees and knows is only near at hand—neither far-sighted nor far-thinking. Therefore, mistakes in planning and errors of judgment will be common. You must be especially careful to avoid being tricked.

THE FORTUNE

Anything you do connected with the arts is favorable. For other things, small things are auspicious, but in large things, the capacity does not match the will. There is a possibility you may be cheated, tricked, or slandered.

Wish: A modest wish will be realized but not wild or extravagant hopes.

Marriage: The other side may be hiding something. You must make an investigation and decide after everything is clear or in the open.

Love: Success is possible, but as hopes are set too high disappointment will follow.

Family: The exterior is deceptive—poverty and distress are on the inside. You must abandon vanity, ostentation, luxury, and extravagance in order to secure the family fortunes.

Children: It appears that the children are sickly and weak. Pregnancy: girl.

Capital loans: A small loan is possible but not a large one.

Business: Success and profit.

Stock market: A false boom; prices will soon drop.

Life span: Weak constitution. If you do not regulate and discipline yourself, you possibly will lead a short life.

Sickness: More serious than it appears on the surface. Take care in treating your health, otherwise your life may even be in danger.

Waiting for someone: This person will come, but will bring disappointment.

Looking for someone: This person will return soon or his whereabouts will become known. This person might be hiding or staying in the house of a friend or a relative to the south or northeast.

Lost article: Mistakenly placed in something. Look to the south or northeast.

Travel: A short trip is propitious but not a long one.

Lawsuit and disputes: Adversity; but a compromise is possible.

Employment: Can be found; but if conditions are set too high, the result will be failure.

Examination: Good score.

New business, change of occupation or specialization, and moving: Propitious.

Weather: Clear, but will soon turn cloudy.

H E X A G R A M   2 3

PO

bo

Splitting apart

	Primary	Upper	Ken	Keeping Still
		Lower	K'un	Receptive
	Nuclear	Above	K'un	Receptive
		Below	K'un	Receptive

Po means to cut down, split apart, strip, denude, or flay. Looking at the hexagram, we see that *yin* or broken lines dominate going up, with but one *yang* or solid line left. It appears as though the *yang* force is tottering and ready to fall. The upper trigram *Ken* represents the mountains and the lower trigram *K'un* the earth. The towering mountain is unable to withstand the encroachment of the wind and rain, gradually collapsing and washing away, being made level. In divining, this hexagram means that your luck is at its lowest ebb. The only thing to do is to maintain the status quo and wait for a change for the better.

THE FORTUNE

Your luck is down. Distress, poverty, or a decline in business or career is possible. Moreover, you may even become involved in a love affair, betrayed, slandered, or harmed by someone, thereby losing money, property, and the like. You must be cautious and even retreat to maintain your position.

Wish: Will not be realized.

Marriage: A bad match. If you do get married, the husband will die first. You cannot fully believe or trust the matchmaker, go-between, or the one who made the introduction.

Love: Will end in tragedy or refusal by the other party, perhaps in even being driven away.

Family: Fortunes declining. In addition, members of the family and relatives are devoid of emotions for each other. You must patiently and quietly endure hardships and bitterness in order for the family to regain good fortune.

Children: No children, weak and sickly children, or incompatibility between children and parents. Pregnancy: girl.

Capital loan: Unsuccessful.

Business: Failure and loss. It is best to retreat and wait for a better opportunity.

Stock market: Recession.

Life span: Sickly and a short life. Attention must be paid to disciplining yourself.

Sickness: If there is danger, then death is a certainty. Venereal disease, peritonitis, tuberculosis, lung ailments, and head diseases.

Waiting for someone: Will not come. If this person should come, he will bring trouble.

Looking for someone: This person has left because of some failure, money problems, or love affair. Look for this person to the northeast or southwest in mountains or by some water's edge; you may not be able to find him.

Lost article: Stolen or lost. You will not get it back.

Travel: Trouble may occur midway in the journey. Best not to go on this journey.

Lawsuit and disputes: Crushing or ignominious defeat.

Employment: For the moment, no hope.

Examination: Very poor score.

New business, change of occupation or specialization, and moving: Adverse. It is not favorable to proceed with plans.

Weather: Continuous bad weather.

FU

fu

Return (The turning point)

	Primary	Upper	K'un	Receptive
		Lower	Chen	Arousing
	Nuclear	Above	K'un	Receptive
		Below	K'un	Receptive

Fu means to return to the original and to begin anew. The *yang* force, represented by the solid bottom line, is moving upwards, rising from the bottom. The *yang* force is therefore beginning to move and myriad things are receiving vitality from this force, gradually gaining power. In divination, it means that things are turning for the better—as though spring were about to arrive. Things will become progressively better.

THE FORTUNE

Recently your luck has been bad or just so-so. But now good fortune is approaching. Proceed carefully with measured steps and in logical order; all will turn for the better. Do not act rashly or impulsively. This hexagram also suggests the beginning of the success of your plans.

Wish: Success soon. Do not be impatient or impulsive.

Marriage: Success will come with perseverance. A good match that will gradually reap blessings and joy. A remarriage, i.e., a second or more, is also propitious.

Love: Success through sincerity and perseverance. It is possible the young man may have many girlfriends.

Family: The dawning of prosperity and good fortune.

Children: Many children, more boys than girls. In the future, success and achievements for your son(s). Pregnancy: boy.

Capital loans: Success soon.

Business: Poor recently, but will gradually improve.

Stock market: Prices are gradually rising.

Life span: While young, somewhat weak and prone to illness. Gradually healthier and healthier—a long life.

Sickness: Treatment will take considerable time, but recovery is certain. Diseases of the stomach and bowels, neuralgia.

Waiting for someone: Will come, but late.

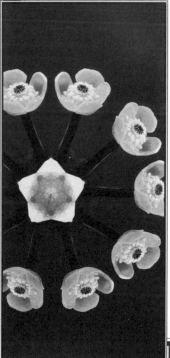

Looking for someone: In seven days this person will return on his own or his whereabouts will become known. Look in the east or southwest.

Lost article: It can be found, but you must search patiently. Search in the east or southwest.

Travel: Propitious.

Lawsuit and disputes: Lengthy and time-consuming but in the end it will be resolved in your favor.

Employment: No problem, but you must wait a few days.

Examination: Progress; score has somewhat improved.

New business, change of occupation or specialization, and moving: Propitious.

Weather: Good weather will gradually return.

WU WANG

wu wang

Innocent (The unexpected)

	Primary	Upper	Ch'ien	Creative
		Lower	Chen	Arousing
	Nuclear	Above	Sun	Gentle
		Below	Ken	Keeping Still

Wu Wang has the meaning of following naturally, of not being in the least bit forced. *Ch'ien*, the upper trigram, stands for heaven while the lower trigram *Chen* represents thunder. *Chen* also suggests dynamism. *Wu Wang* symbolizes the moving in orbit of the ways of heaven, i.e., natural laws. Thus there are four distinct seasons and myriad objects grow and mature naturally, not artificially. In divining, it means that this is the time to let things take their natural course—let it be. Do not take positive action, yet do not shirk from doing what you are supposed to do. Responsibilities must still be fulfilled.

THE FORTUNE

Do not be infatuated with gaining personal advantage or satisfying personal desires or pleasures; otherwise you will meet with misfortune. Deal with people and handle affairs with utmost sincerity. It is auspicious for you to follow along naturally, maintaining your position. Positive action—that is, vigorous, even radical movement—will end in adversity.

Wish: Proper action or behavior according to the norm will lead to success. Shortcuts or unorthodox maneuvers will lead to failure.

Marriage: Success through candidness, honesty, and sincerity. If married couples treat each other with sincerity, then happiness and blessings will be theirs forever.

Love: Success depends on a mutual attitude of honesty and sincerity.

Family: Smooth good fortune.

Children: Many children and good fortune. But you must not spoil them, forgetting their training and education and thereby harming them. Pregnancy: boy.

Capital loan: Realization of the amount desired is possible. However unorthodox methods will lead to failure.

Business: Honest business practices will lead to profits. If you contemplate great profits, you will inevitably encounter failure or loss.

Stock market: Prices rising.

Life span: Naturally healthy. Will lead a long life.

Sickness: Care in convalescence will lead to recovery. To disregard recuperatory treatment will lead to misfortune. Diseases of the organs and the respiratory system and nervous disorders.

Waiting for someone: This person will come.

Looking for someone: Far away. Search to the east or northwest.

Lost article: Left because of something to do with a woman. Hiding in a dark and narrow place. Eventually will be found.

Travel: Possible.

Lawsuit and disputes: If you have reason on your side you will be victorious. An unreasonable or illogical case will lead to defeat.

Employment: You will find a job if you search with sincerity.

Examination: Earnest diligence will lead to good scores. Guessing at problems will end in failure.

New business, change of occupation or specialization, and moving: Do not force it. Natural developments are auspicious.

Weather: Clear and later cloudy. Windy.

HEXAGRAM 26

TA CH'U

da chu

The taming power of the great

Primary	*Upper*	*Ken*	*Keeping Still*
	Lower	*Chien*	*Creative*
Nuclear	*Above*	*Chen*	*Arousing*
	Below	*Tui*	*Joyous*

Ta Ch'u means accumulation, saving, or storing up. At the same time it means fullness or abundance. It also suggests stopping and waiting until full before initiation action. The upper trigram *Ken* means motionlessness, standing still, or rest. The lower trigram *Ch'ien* suggests strength and forward motion. In the hexagram, however, this motion is stopped by the force of *Ken.* It thus rests there filling itself and assembling or gathering itself together. In divining, it means that your wealth, power, knowledge and the like are in the process of maturing, filling up, and improving. They will be brought into full play later.

THE FORTUNE

For the moment stoppage and setbacks, things not going as you hoped. But if you do not regard hard work as toil and keep yourself calm and cool, you will overcome difficulties in the near future and realize your goal. This hexagram also suggests that you may be able to save some money, carry out some business operation, attain the backing or liking of a superior, receive a promotion, or improve in your studies.

Wish: For the moment, trouble. But if you do not act impulsively or rashly, success will gradually be realized.

Marriage: Positive action will lead to success. Both sides are serious about life and love.

Love: Opposition will come from the older generation or some third party. Remain firm and steadfast and success will be yours.

Family: At first, hardships, but if you stick steadfastly to the proper path and earnestly move forward, the family fortunes will gradually change. Inheritance possible. Success is also possible by going out alone to start a new life in strange surroundings.

Children: Their involvements will cause you distress, but eventually you will see them successful and happy. Pregnancy: boy.

Capital loan: For the moment difficulties, but you will gradually succeed.

Business: Substantial profits in 30 days at the earliest and three months at the latest.

Stock market: Prices will drop for some time yet, and then they will rise.

Life span: Many illnesses while young. Later healthy and a long life.

Sickness: Serious and lengthy. Diseases of the chest and belly.

Waiting for someone: For the moment he will not come, but after a certain length of time he will come.

Looking for someone: It will take time. After you spend considerable time searching, this person will either return voluntarily or you will find him. Search to the northwest or northeast.

Lost article: Misplaced under something. It will take time but you will find it. Look to the northeast.

Travel: Sudden and unexpected obstacles.

Lawsuit and disputes: Troublesome and time-consuming but eventually you will gain victory or a favorable outcome.

Employment: It will take time but sooner or later you will obtain a good position.

Examination: Good scores.

New business, change of occupation or specialization, and moving: Propitious.

Weather: Very bad, but will clear soon.

yi

The corners of the mouth (Providing nourishment)

Primary	Upper	Ken	Keeping Still
	Lower	Chen	Arousing
Nuclear	Above	K'un	Receptive
	Below	K'un	Receptive

I means the cheeks and also nourishment. Nourishment comes in the form of the nutrition of food, the absorbing of knowledge and learning, the development of thoughts, and the cultivation of one's person. The top and bottom lines of the hexagram are *yang* or solid and resemble the upper and lower lips. The four *yin* or broken lines in the middle represent the teeth. Good food will nourish the body, but the wrong or spoiled food will harm the body. Likewise with learning and thoughts, what is accepted must be correct. In divining, it means that if one is cautious and careful in his speech, regulates what he eats or drinks, cultivates his person, and treats others or handles affairs according to the correct way, then good fortune will open up. If not, failure will come.

THE FORTUNE

Impulsive actions will lead to defeat. You must maintain the correct path, cultivate your character and your capabilities in order to achieve success.

Careless words and deeds may bring you misfortune. Sickness may come from lack of proper care of your health. Your subordinates may involve you in something. Cooperative ventures are somewhat more auspicious than others.

Wish: Realization after initial difficulties.

Marriage: Make a detailed investigation of the health of the other party before deciding whether to proceed. Success depends on good faith between the two parties.

Love: You have already reached the dating stage—movies, coffee, meals, dancing, etc. Emotions and feelings may obscure judgment. You may be setting your sights too high. Calm down and make a new, clear-headed evaluation.

Family: Time of decline. Honor and name lost, bankruptcy—time for bitterness. You must calmly evaluate the situation and your own words and deeds and plan to reverse the family fortunes.

Children: Pampering the children has harmed them. You must examine your actions and words and change the method used to train and educate your children. Pregnancy: girl.

Capital loan: Success after initial difficulties.

Business: Thoroughly investigate business opportunities and act with the utmost honesty. Do not be devious or greedy. Profit will then be yours.

Stock market: Prices low, will rise later.

Life span: Excessive eating and drinking will harm your health and cause a short life. Lead a regulated daily life and pay attention to your body—you can then attain good health.

Sickness: Dangerous. Special care must be taken in convalescing. Afflicted parts—stomach and bowels, teeth, and throat.

Waiting for someone: Will not come.

Looking for someone: Not far off, hiding or staying somewhere nearby. Search from the east to the northeast.

Lost article: Misplaced indoors. Underneath something. Look from the east to the northeast.

Travel: Not very good at the beginning, but much much better later.

Lawsuit and disputes: Adversity; best to seek a compromise.

Employment: Strive hard and success will be yours.

Examination: Good score.

New business, change of occupation or specialization, and moving: Not the right time. Wait for a better moment.

Weather: Cloudy.

H E X A G R A M   2 8

TA KUO

da guo

Preponderance of the great

	Primary	Upper	Tui	Joyous
		Lower	Sun	Gentle
	Nuclear	Above	Chien	Creative
		Below	Chien	Creative

Ta Kuo means excess or excessive strength. The upper trigram is *Tui*, representing marshes, and the lower trigram is *Sun*, standing for trees. Too much water has inundated the trees, causing them to die. In divining, it means that your burdens and responsibilities are too heavy. Your strength does not match your will—an exceptionally distressing situation.

THE FORTUNE

As your burdens and responsibilities are too heavy, you will be unable to completely carry them out or fulfill them, thereby meeting setbacks. You should evaluate your strengths and weaknesses and select an appropriate course of action. Perhaps then your luck will change. You may become involved in complications, your body and mind upset and disturbed. Or you may be the victim of some error in documentation or encounter a flood. Rash and blind actions will bring you defeat.

Wish: Hopes set too high. They will not be realized.

Marriage: An ill match. Even if a marriage takes place there will be no feelings between husband and wife, or the two will be separated in life and parted at death—bitterness and sorrow.

Love: Already intimate. Cannot part from each other even though the other party is not suited for you.

Family: Declining fortunes and trouble and hardship. You must renovate household affairs and reduce expenditures before your fortunes can be reversed.

Children: Many children. Their upbringing will be difficult. There is a lack of understanding or forgiveness between parents and children. You must persevere in striving to teach and guide them. When this is done, happiness and blessings will be yours. Pregnancy: boy.

Capital loan: It appears as though success is highly possible, but all is empty talk. Realization will be very difficult.

Business: Prices high but situation unstable. Sell fast and you may reap a profit.

Stock market: Prices high. Big drop in a few days.

Life span: Naturally healthy. But there is a possibility that you will strain yourself by overworking, causing illness and even an early death. Avoid excessive work and toil and you will protect yourself; you may even enjoy a long life.

Sickness: Serious but not hopeless. Afflicted areas: the spinal cord and the lungs.

Waiting for someone: Will not come.

Looking for someone: Far away. It will not be easy to find the whereabouts of this person. Look to the west or southeast.

Lost article: Not easily found.

Travel: Obstacles and dangers possible. Best to abandon this journey.

Lawsuit and disputes: Defeat possible. Best to seek a compromise.

Employment: Difficulties.

Examination: Difficult questions will cause you worry.

New business, change of occupation or specialization, and moving: Difficulties at first but after a period of time things will be all right.

Weather: Cloudy at dawn and dusk, clearing in between.

H E X A G R A M 2 9

K'AN

kan

The abysmal (Water)

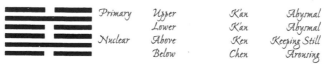

Primary	Upper	K'an	Abysmal
	Lower	K'an	Abysmal
Nuclear	Above	Ken	Keeping Still
	Below	Chen	Arousing

Both upper and lower trigrams are *K'an*. Thus the hexagram is also called *K'an*. *K'an* means trouble and danger and stands for water. Water above and below suggests that the water's depth cannot be discerned. Vast and restless, colliding and flowing—the image is of exceptional danger. Drowning is a possibility. In divining, it means that your luck is extremely bad, as if involved in a double bind when it is both dangerous to go forward and to retreat.

THE FORTUNE
Many hardships and difficulties. You must have firm convictions and not fear trouble. The only thing to do is wait for your luck to change. You cannot advance and you cannot retreat. You will perhaps be disquieted in body and soul, not being able to dwell in ease. Drifting about, you may encounter robbery, be cheated, take sick, or become injured.

Wish: Many difficulties, cannot be realized.

Marriage: Not an ideal match. Trouble on both sides makes success difficult. The male may be marrying for his second or more time and is not of one mind about his love. However, the remarriage of an older person is auspicious.

Love: Many ordeals and anguish. Success is very difficult.

Family: Many troubles. You must bear them with patience. There may be a turn for the better. The possibility also exists that the family will split up because of disharmony.

Children: Your children will cause you anxiety. Hard work in rearing them will bring the hope of their future success. Pregnancy: boy, but delivery may be difficult.

Capital loan: Difficulties will make success impossible.

Business: Not smooth. But do not act impulsively or rashly. Wait for a better moment.

Stock market: Prices dropping.

Life span: Weak and sickly, a short life. You must pay attention to disciplining yourself.

Sickness: Very serious; death is a distinct possibility. Heart attacks, kidney diseases, or peritonitis.

Waiting for someone: Will not come. He may come after a very long time.

Looking for someone: In danger now. Left because of disharmony at home or because he could not get his way. Look to the north.

Lost article: Misplaced or stolen. You will not find it or get it back.

Travel: Should not travel, for you will encounter trouble if you do.

Lawsuit and disputes: Lengthy, time-consuming, and not advantageous.

Employment: No hope for the time being.

Examination: Very poor score.

New business, change of occupation or specialization, and moving: Adversity. Wait for a better moment.

Weather: A succession of rainy days.

HEXAGRAM 30

LI

li

The clinging, fire

Primary	Upper	Li	Clinging
	Lower	Li	Clinging
Nuclear	Above	Tui	Joyous
	Lower	Sun	Gentle

As both upper and lower trigrams are *Li*, the hexagram is called *Li*. *Li* means brightness, brilliance, and beauty, and symbolizes the sun and fire. The shape of the hexagram suggests that one sun has just set and another rises immediately to shine brightly over a myriad of things, causing everything to flourish and prosper and making beautiful scenery appear. In divining, it means that like the sun moving on high, everything will go smoothly for honest and upright people. But for the perverse and those whose hearts are not honest and just, failure is a certainty.

THE FORTUNE

Good fortune is yours if you keep to the correct path, remain humble and obliging, have respect for the opinions of others, and unite with others in doing things. Cooperative ventures will succeed. It is auspicious to follow the opinions of your elders. If you are impulsive, rash, shortsighted, or swayed by emotion in handling affairs, you will meet defeat.

Wish: Success will be yours if you go forward with sincerity. You may be aided by someone else.

Marriage: A good match. Entrust someone with position to act as go-between. Continue contact and success is yours.

Love: Both sides are passionate, but rash and impulsive actions will lead to failure.

Family: Prosperous and happy. However, haughtiness and conceit will lead to destroying the good fortune.

Children: Many children and blessings. Pregnancy: girl.

Capital loan: Success through the aid of a third party.

Business: You can reap a profit.

Stock market: Rising or will rise soon.

Life span: Healthy and long life.

Sickness: Serious. Recovery through careful convalescence. Fevers, eye diseases, or diseases in the abdominal region.

Waiting for someone: Will come.

Looking for someone: Enticed or incited to leave home. Look to the south.

Lost article: Attached or sticking to something. If you look hard you will find it. Look to the south.

Travel: Propitious.

Lawsuit and disputes: If reason is on your side or if the other party uses unscrupulous methods, then victory is yours. The opposite will lead to defeat.

Employment: Place your faith in the older generation and wait for the time to mature and a good job will be yours.

Examination: Good score.

New business, change of occupation or specialization, and moving: With full and complete preparations, you may proceed. Carelessness will surely lead to failure.

Weather: Clear, very hot.

HEXAGRAM 31

HSIEN

xian

Influence (Wooing)

Primary	Upper	Tui	Joyous
	Lower	Ken	Keeping Still
Nuclear	Above	Chien	Creative
	Below	Sun	Gentle

Hsien has the meaning of to feel and respond—mutual influence. All things in the world have mutual feelings or sympathetic vibrations, the most obvious being the mutual response of feelings between men and women. The upper trigram is *Tui*, symbolizing young women, and the lower trigram is *Ken*, symbolizing young men and youth. The young man

164

is below the young woman—there is contact and response. *Tui* also stands for joy and happiness, while *Ken* represents quietude and cessation. The hexagram thus suggests the peace and quiet that comes from the contentment that follows happiness or joy. In divining, it means that all will go as hoped and that there will be happiness. However, you must avoid the perverse and the incorrect, for such interaction causes contamination.

THE FORTUNE

Good fortune—everything going as you hope. Cooperative ventures are auspicious. Nevertheless, the possibility exists that you may become involved in sexual complications or make the wrong friends and mistakenly enter the path of evil or incorrectness.

Wish: Can be realized.

Marriage: Smooth going; a good match.

Love: You have already reached a considerable degree of affection. Success is definite.

Family: Harmonious and flourishing household.

Children: Harmonious feeling between children and parents. Spoiling the children, however, will ruin this fortunate circumstance. Pregnancy: girl.

Capital loan: Success.

Business: Profits will be realized as hoped.

Stock market: Situation stable.

Life span: Healthy and long life.

Sickness: Will recover. Venereal diseases and diseases of the chest region.

Waiting for someone: Will come, bringing joy and laughter.

Looking for someone: This person is involved in some sort of sexual complication. Can be found soon.

Lost article: Mixed into something else or mistakenly placed into something. Look in the northeast or west.

Travel: You will meet someone on the journey. You must guard against illicit love.

Lawsuit and disputes: Adverse. Best to compromise.

Employment: No difficulties.

Examination: Very good score.

New business, change of occupation or specialization, and moving: Can proceed.

Weather: Rainy.

HEXAGRAM 32

HENG

heng

Duration

	Primary	Upper	Chen	Arousing
		Lower	Sun	Gentle
	Nuclear	Above	Tui	Joyous
		Below	Chien	Creative

Heng means duration and unchangeable constancy. The upper trigram is *Chen*, which stands for the eldest son, while the lower trigram is *Sun*, standing for the eldest daughter. The male is in the position above the female, meaning union. For couples it means that the way of marriage is to grow old and white-haired together. Your present position should be maintained and new plans avoided. In this way trouble-free and long-lasting good fortune can be obtained.

THE FORTUNE

Honesty, sincerity, and guarding your position carefully will mean that everything will go smoothly and that you can maintain prosperity.

Wish: Success possible.

Marriage: Durable, compatible, good match. Trouble-free success.

Love: Durable emotions.

Family: Born in a large family. Lasting good fortune.

Children: Compatibility between parents and children. Peace and happiness. Pregnancy: boy. Safe delivery.

Capital loan: Success.

Business: Smooth profits.

Stock market: Rising, but there is a limit to the rise.

Life span: Healthy and long life.

Sickness: Time-consuming, but recovery is possible. Chronic diseases.

Waiting for someone: Will come.

Looking for someone: It will take time, but this person will either return safe and sound or his whereabouts will become known.

Lost article: Indoors. Search patiently and you will find it. Look to the southeast.

Travel: Propitious.

Lawsuit and disputes: Adverse. Should seek a compromise.

Employment: You will find very suitable work.

Examination: You will maintain very good scores.

New business, change of occupation or specialization, and moving: Not propitious. Best to maintain your present position.

Weather: Clear and windy.

TUN

dun

Retreat

	Primary	Upper	Ch'ien	Creative
		Lower	Ken	Keeping Still
	Nuclear	Above	Ch'ien	Creative
		Below	Sun	Gentle

Tun means to retreat, withdraw, or flee. The bottom two lines are *yin* or broken lines while the top four lines are *yang* or solid lines, meaning that the *yin* force is gradually ascending while the *yang* force is retreating. In divining, it means that a decline in fortunes has begun and that it is auspicious to retreat and not to advance.

THE FORTUNE

A premonition of declining fortunes. In all matters retreat and hold that position. Be extremely cautious in words, deeds, and handling affairs and you can be safe and sound. You may be slandered by petty people, be involved in complications by your subordinates, and lose property or wealth.

Wish: Not successful.

Marriage: Cannot get together. Even if you do marry, the match will not be compatible.

Love: Personalities are not matched. Moreover, the girl may have another man in mind.

Family: The trend is for declining fortunes and ill luck.

Children: The children are not loyal. Moreover, they are neither healthy nor strong. Pregnancy: boy.

Capital loan: Unsuccessful.

Business: Losses and failure. Best to stop temporarily.

Stock market: Falling prices.

Life span: Weak and unhealthy—a short life. You must regulate your life in order to promote good health.

Sickness: Very serious. Best to go somewhere else to recover. Diseases of the chest, abdomen, and the bone marrow.

Waiting for someone: Will not come.

Looking for someone: This person left because of dissipation, lack of ambition, or family chaos. He is far away and you cannot find him.

Lost article: Already fallen into someone else's hands and you will not get it back.

Travel: Many hindrances and difficulties. Be careful to avoid disaster. In some cases travel will be impossible.

Lawsuit and disputes: Defeat. Best to drop it.

Employment: Hopeless.

Examination: Very poor score.

New business, change of occupation or specialization, and moving: Not the right time; advancement cannot succeed. Nonetheless, positive steps may be taken in the entertainment business—theaters, hotels, drinking establishments, etc.

Weather: Gradually worsening.

HEXAGRAM 34

TA CHUANG

da zhuang

The power of the great

Primary	*Upper*	*Chen*	*Arousing*
	Lower	*Chien*	*Creative*
Nuclear	*Above*	*Tui*	*Joyous*
	Below	*Chien*	*Creative*

Ta Chuang means that the *yang* force is especially strong and prosperous or heroic, virile, and imposing. The bottom four *yang* or solid lines are ascending, causing the top two *yin* or broken lines to retreat. Thus it symbolizes that influence, power, and prestige cannot be blocked or stopped. The upper trigram is *Chen*, representing thunder, and the lower trigram is *Ch'ien*, representing heaven. Thunder in the heavens resounds with unmatched strength, imposing and majestic. In divining, it means that prosperous or flourishing fortunes are here. But excess or an unyielding or obstinate stand in any matter will bring about misfortune. You must be cautious.

THE FORTUNE

Fortunes flourishing, business expanding. But there is a possibility that in handling affairs a lack of friendliness or cordiality will lead to conflict and excited, impulsive actions to loss or failure. You may offend or harm some person because of an intolerant attitude. You must be open-minded and modest in treating others or in handling affairs.

Wish: Success.

Marriage: Can succeed; a well-suited match that will be happy and full of blessings. Husband and wife must be amiable and follow propriety in order not to destroy the good fortune.

Love: Pressing too hard will lead to failure. Take a step back and treat the other party well. Treat the other party with attention every day and success will be yours.

Family: Happiness and well-being. Haughtiness will lead to disharmony in the family and even insolvency.

Children: The children may be stubborn. This can lead to disharmony in the family. In rearing them, correct this flaw and they will be successful and happy. Pregnancy: boy.

Capital loan: Your goal will be realized.

Business: Success and great profits.

Stock market: Prices rising.

Life span: Naturally healthy, should live a long life. Nonetheless, you must take care of your body.

Sickness: Heretofore healthy. If you adhere to the methods of rest and recuperation you can recover. Acute pneumonia or diseases of the brain.

Waiting for someone: Will come soon.

Looking for someone: Far away. Very difficult to find out the whereabouts of this person.

Lost article: Can be found. Look to the northeast in a high place.

Travel: Proceed but be careful en route.

Lawsuit and disputes: Victory.

Employment: Success possible.

Examination: Good score.

New business, change of occupation or specialization, and moving: Proceed.

Weather: Clear.

H E X A G R A M   3 5

CHIN

jin

Progress

Primary	Upper	Li	Clinging
	Lower	K'un	Receptive
Nuclear	Above	K'an	Abysmal
	Below	Ken	Keeping Still

Chin means to go forward, advance, proceed, and progress. The upper trigram is *Li*, representing the sun, and the lower trigram is *K'un*, representing the earth. The sun is above the earth as in the morning when it rises, casting its brilliance out over the world. The sunrise is also the start of a new day and suggests the beginning of movement and action. *Li* also means brightness and *K'un* implies yielding, submission, following, or obedience. Hence, by submitting to brightness, clear development or progress is achieved. In divining, it means that like the sun rising in the east and myriad things beginning to develop, your fortune is opening up and all will go as hoped.

THE FORTUNE

Great, prosperous, good fortune. You may be assisted by some person or by your elder. Prosperity in business and a gradual rise in reputation, everything going as hoped. It is also suitable to cooperate with others. However, someone may be envious of you.

Wish: Success.

Marriage: Propitious. You may be assisted by some woman older than you.

Love: Success certain.

Family: Prosperous family, increasingly flourishing.

Children: Intelligent and talented. Moreover they are obedient and loyal. Pregnancy: girl.

Capital loan: Success.

Business: Smooth going and good profit.

Stock market: Rising prices.

Life span: Healthy and long life.

Sickness: Recovery possible in near future. Diseases of the stomach and bowels, and diabetes.

Waiting for someone: Will come, bringing good news.

Looking for someone: Far away but will return soon or soon be found. Look to the south or southwest.

Lost article: You can find it. Search in the south or southwest.

Travel: Propitious. Destination or purpose of travel will be reached.

Lawsuit and disputes: Victory.

Employment: Success through the assistance of someone of the older generation.

Examination: Good score.

New business, change of occupation or specialization, and moving: Greatly propitious.

Weather: Fine and clear.

HEXAGRAM 3 6

MING I

ming yi

Darkening of the light

Primary	Upper	K'un	Receptive
	Lower	Li	Clinging
Nuclear	Above	Chen	Arousing
	Below	K'an	Abysmal

Ming I means the extinguishing of light or brilliance. The upper trigram is *K'un* or earth, and the lower trigram is *Li* or the sun. The sun has descended below the earth, causing darkness. *Li* also stands for fire. Fire in the distance casts its light far and wide. In this case, however, the opposite is true. The fire is below the earth and therefore suggests darkness. In divining, it means that like a dark night the future is unclear, so caution is advised until the sky lightens in the morning. Wait patiently until the light comes again before taking action or moving forward.

THE FORTUNE

Bad luck, hardship, and toil. Someone may be jealous of you or cheat you. You may be injured or encounter a fire or robbery. You must be extremely cautious and wait patiently with self-discipline for your luck to change.

Wish: Unsuccessful.

Marriage: A bad match. Even if married the marriage will break up. However, you may proceed with a secret marriage or elopement.

Love: Large obstacles mean no success.

Family: Declining fortunes. Frequent friction and conflict within.

Children: Your children's involvements will make you suffer. Attention and efforts in training and educating your children will mean hope for future success and well-being. Pregnancy: girl. Possibility of a difficult delivery.

Capital loan: Unsuccessful.

Business: Rough going, even losses. Best to stop temporarily.

Stock market: Prices falling

Life span: Weak, sickly, with the possibility of a short life. You must take care to discipline yourself.

Sickness: Serious but not fatal. Latent or hidden diseases are a possibility. Diseases of the abdominal region.

Waiting for someone: Will not come.

Looking for someone: Hiding nearby. Look to the southwest or south.

Lost article: Misplaced underneath something. Search in the southwest or south.

Travel: Calamity possible midway. Best to stop this trip.

Lawsuit and disputes: Defeat. Jail or prison a possibility.

Employment: No hope for the present.

Examination: Poor score.

New business, change of occupation or specialization, and moving: Adversity. Wait for your luck to change.

Weather: Continuous bad weather.

HEXAGRAM 37

jia ren

The family (The clan)

	Primary	Upper	Sun	Gentle
		Lower	Li	Clinging
	Nuclear	Above	Li	Clinging
		Below	K'an	Abysmal

Chia Jen means the family or members of the family. It also can be explained as family livelihood and family possessions. It is a human and social constant that the man works or fights on the outside while the woman stays inside, managing household affairs. In this hexagram the fifth line (second line from the top) is a solid *yang* line, occupying the middle position of the upper trigram. The second line from the bottom is a broken or *yin* line and occupies the middle position of the lower trigram. As both are in their proper position, the hexagram has the meaning of family constancy—the husband working on the outside and the wife managing family affairs at home. The upper trigram *Sun* stands for the eldest daughter while the lower trigram *Li* stands for the middle daughter. The older precedes the younger, maintaining the proper sequence between seniors and juniors. In divining, this hexagram means that the family is on the proper path and flourishing.

THE FORTUNE

Great good fortune filled with joy. Do your duty and work hard without any extraneous plans or impulsive actions. In this way you can maintain your good fortune.

Wish: Can be realized.

Marriage: A compatible and fortunate match—success.

Love: Success is possible.

Family: Peace, harmony, and well-being. The family fortune is flourishing. Great good fortune.

Children: Children are all obedient and loyal. The image is one of many children. Pregnancy: girl.

Capital loans: You will realize only a small part of what you hope for.

Business: Smooth going and profits. But do not expand.

Stock market: Prices will rise for the time being, but will fall later.

Life span: A healthy and long life.

Sickness: Not serious. Recovery will come soon. Heavy colds and intestinal or bowel inflammations.

Waiting for someone: Will come bringing good news.

Looking for someone: Do not worry. This person will soon return voluntarily.

Lost article: Lost indoors. Will be found soon. Look to the south or southeast.

Travel: Propitious. A safe and sound journey.

Lawsuit and disputes: Compromise will bring about a resolution.

Employment: No difficulties.

Examination: Good score.

New business, change of occupation or specialization, and moving: Action that brings about change is not suitable at the moment. It is best to maintain your present situation.

Weather: Clear and windy.

HEXAGRAM 38

K'UEI

kui

Opposition

	Primary	Upper	Li	Clinging
		Lower	Tui	Joyous
	Nuclear	Above	K'an	Abysmal
		Below	Li	Clinging

K'uei symbolizes disunion and opposition. The upper trigram *Li* is fire and the lower trigram *Tui* is marshes. Fire burns upward and the water of the marsh flows downward. The two trigrams are thus in opposition and disharmony. In divining, the hexagram means that ideas are not in agreement and nothing is easily accomplished.

THE FORTUNE

Rough going. Difficulties will dominate all affairs and expectations will be disappointed. Avoid forward movement or advancement. Hold your position and amiably carry out your affairs. Danger can then be changed to security and peace. You may become involved in some complication involving others, make faulty plans, or alienate a friend.

Wish: Realization is extremely difficult.

Marriage: Family opposition will lead to failure. If the marriage does take place, differing interests and pursuits will lead to separation.

Love: Dissimilar personalities will lead to a parting.

Family: Disharmony. Family fortunes declining. Hardship and bitterness.

Children: The image is the lack of feelings between parents and children. Pregnancy: girl. The delivery may be difficult.

Capital loans: Realization difficult.

Business: Many obstacles. Disharmony between partners may mean faulty planning and losses or failure of some kind.

Stock market: Prices falling.

Life span: Many illnesses and a possibility of a short life.

Sickness: Very serious. The doctor may make a mistake in treatment. Afflictions or malfunction of internal organs.

Waiting for someone: Will not come.

Looking for someone: A quarrel or difference of opinion caused this person to leave. It is not easy to find his whereabouts.

Lost article: Already in someone else's hands. It will not be returned.

Travel: Obstacles will prevent you from realizing the goal or purpose of the journey. Best to stop plans to travel.

Lawsuit and disputes: Adverse. Best to seek a compromise.

Employment: No hope.

Examination: Poor score. Beware of misunderstanding the wording of questions or doing the wrong problems.

New business, change of occupation or specialization, and moving: Adverse. If you proceed you will not realize your hopes.

Weather: Cloudy.

HEXAGRAM 39

CHIEN

jian

Obstruction

	Primary	Upper	K'an	Abysmal
		Lower	Ken	Keeping Still
	Nuclear	Above	Li	Clinging
		Below	K'an	Abysmal

Chien symbolizes difficulty in action and inhibition. It also means great difficulty, distress, trouble, and hardship. The upper trigram *K'an* symbolizes danger while the lower trigram *Ken* symbolizes cessation of movement. The hexagram thus means being stopped in danger with no way out. *K'an* also stands for water and *Ken* for mountains, suggesting that the way is blocked by dangerous waters on the one hand and tall mountains on the other. In divining, it means being in a dilemma where both forward and backward movement are difficult. In this case, this period of hardship must be passed through with extreme caution.

THE FORTUNE

The fortune is obstructed and there are hardships and distress. Wait patiently with self-discipline, follow talented and virtuous elders, and improve yourself. In five months at the earliest or five years at the latest your luck will change. Development to the southwest may be possible but adversity will meet advances in the northeast. You may encounter a robbery, be cheated, encounter a flood, or be stabbed in the back by a subordinate or a close friend.

Wish: Will not be realized.

Marriage: Not fated for each other. Best to find another mate. Possibility of a many-sided love affair.

Love: Complications and failure.

Family: Poverty, distress, and no emotional attachments among family members. You must strive hard to turn back the tide of adversity.

Children: The children will cause toil and pain for their parents. Moreover, there are no feelings between children and parents. Pregnancy: boy. Possibility of a difficult delivery.

Capital loan: Failure.

Business: Many problems, with the outcome of loss or failure. Best to stop temporarily.

Stock market: Depressed prices to continue.

Life span: Sickly and weak. Possibility of a short life exists. You must make efforts at self-discipline.

Sickness: Serious and dangerous. Care in recuperation will mean recovery. Peritonitis and diseases of the kidneys, liver, and chest region.

Waiting for someone: Will not come.

Looking for someone: Disappointments and poverty have caused this person to leave. There is a possibility of danger. If in five months this person is not found, then there is no hope. Search to the north and northeast.

Lost article: Mistakenly placed into something or mixed up in something. Patient searching will lead to success. Search in the north or northeast.

Travel: Trouble en route.

Lawsuit and disputes: Difficult and time-consuming.

Employment: For the moment no hope.

Examination: Difficult questions and a poor score.

New business, change of occupation and specialization, and moving: Adverse. Wait for another time.

Weather: Continuous bad weather.

HEXAGRAM 40

HSIEH

xie

Deliverance

Primary	Upper	Chen	Arousing
	Lower	K'an	Abysmal
Nuclear	Above	K'an	Abysmal
	Below	Li	Clinging

Hsieh means release, loosening, dispersion and the alleviation of hardship and trouble. The upper trigram *Chen* symbolizes thunder and the lower trigram *K'an* symbolizes rain. Thus the hexagram suggests pent-up emotions shaken and dispersed by the rain and thunder. *K'an* stands for winter and *Chen* for spring. Taken together they suggest withdrawal from winter and the arrival of spring. Severe cold has been dispersed and spring rains are beginning to fall. Warmth is spreading throughout the land and things are joyous, being enriched and given vitality and zest. In divining, it means hardships are decreasing; new movement can begin.

THE FORTUNE

After a long, arduous period, fortunes are beginning to change and move toward the smooth and great path. Take positive action, grasp this opportunity, and struggle for fame and fortune. New action in the southwest is auspicious. A joyous event may take place in the family.

Wish: Success possible. Do not hesitate, thereby missing this good chance.

Marriage: A good match, success possible.

Love: Do not waiver or hesitate. Take positive action and success can be yours.

Family: At first hardship and toil but gradually fortunes will change for the better.

Children: Initially the children will bring entanglements and toil, but later happiness and well-being will be realized. Pregnancy: boy. Safe delivery.

Capital loan: Success possible. You should take positive action.

Business: Profits can be made. Act promptly and positively.

Stock market: For the present, a slight downward trend in prices. Will rise soon.

Life span: Often ill when young but increasingly healthy as time goes on. A long life.

Sickness: Can recover your health. But you cannot be careless. You must seek proper treatment. Neurosis and diseases of the stomach, bowels, and kidneys.

Waiting for someone: Will come with good intentions.

Looking for someone: Whereabouts will be known soon.

Lost article: Can be found. Promptly search to the east or north. If too much time elapses you will not find it.

Travel: Propitious.

Lawsuit and disputes: After some time it will be resolved in your favor.

Employment: Unexpected harvest. You must seize this opportunity.

Examination: Fairly good score.

New business, change of occupation or specialization, and moving: Can initiate immediate action.

Weather: It will rain.

SUN

sun

Decrease

	Primary	Upper	Ken	Keeping Still
		Lower	Tui	Joyous
	Nuclear	Above	K'un	Receptive
		Below	Chen	Arousing

Sun means sacrifice and decrease, lessening, weakening, reduction, and loss. Lines three, four, and five from the bottom are *yin* or broken lines. The *yin* lines are in between *yang* lines and one occupies the line number five position, the position of the ruler, causing the *yang* force to be weakened. The hexagram formed by the nuclear trigrams is *Fu* (Hexagram 24: Return) where the *yang* force is beginning to ascend. It is returning after being eclipsed by the *yin*. In *Sun* this returning force suggests that although sacrifice is a kind of loss, some good or benefit will be gained in return. In divining, it means that while now there is loss or damage, soon the situation will be counterbalanced and compensation will be yours.

THE FORTUNE

Things are not going as hoped and you may even face losses. But gradually this adverse tide will be turned back and little by little the dawning rays of success will come into view. Cooperative ventures are auspicious.

Wish: For the present, success is not possible. Strive hard with concentration and success will come later.

Marriage: Harmonious, good match. Auspicious for the man to marry into the wife's family or for the couple to live with the wife's family.

Love: Sincerity and consistency will bring success.

Family: Family fortunes declining but can be restored with hard work. In the end happiness can be achieved.

Children. You will toil for them. But they are really sincere and loyal and will realize happiness and well-being later. Pregnancy: girl.

Capital loan: For the moment success difficult.

Business: Losses.

Stock market: Prices falling.

Life span: Weak and sickly; but if there is regimen in your life, a healthy, long life can be yours.

Sickness: Serious but convalescence can lead to recovery. Anemia, diseases of the digestive organs, generally weak or sickly condition.

Looking for someone: It will take a lot of time but this person will either return on his own or his whereabouts will become known. Look in the northeast or west.

Waiting for someone: Will come, but late.

Lost article: Not easily found or perhaps impossible to be recovered. Search in the northeast or west.

Travel: If extreme care is taken during the course of the journey, it is all right to travel.

Lawsuit and disputes: Adverse. Best seek a compromise.

Employment: For the moment no success, but you can find a job later.

Examination: Poor score.

New business, change of occupation or specialization, and moving: At first such a move will not be advantageous, but after a period of time you will reap benefits.

Weather: Cloudy with occasional rain.

yi

Increase

Primary	Upper	Sun	Gentle
	Lower	Chen	Arousing
Nuclear	Above	Ken	Keeping Still
	Below	K'un	Receptive

I means to increase, gain, augment—addition. The upper trigram *Sun* symbolizes the wind while the lower trigram *Chen* symbolizes the thunder. Thunder is produced by the yang force while the *yin* force moves the wind. Both are vital and help myriad things to grow and develop, hence the idea of addition. The basic idea of the hexagram is the growing of things, implying that the public good comes first, not the concern for one's personal interests. As in the hexagram with its moving winds above and thunder below, so can all things take positive action and reap results. In divining, it means that with full vigor you can open up the way, thereby gaining something beneficial.

THE FORTUNE

Enjoying smooth good fortune—a good time for initiating action or expanding. Be decisive and march firmly forward. Do not be hesitant. At the same time you must think about others and how they may benefit. If you do, then you will succeed. You might be assisted by someone else. A happy event may occur in your family. Cooperative ventures are auspicious.

Wish: Can be realized.

Marriage: Harmonious and good match. Success definite. However, much idle talk exists so it is best to get married soon.

Love: Both are very thoughtful and considerate. Success inevitable.

Family: Flourishing and prosperous family fortunes. However, carelessness, excesses, and haughtiness can ruin the good fortune.

Children: Happy and fine children. Pregnancy: girl.

Capital loan: Success possible.

Business: Great profits possible.

Stock market: Prices rising, but be careful for they will fall after a while.

Life span: A healthy and long life.

Sickness: Recovery possible. Stomach ailments, venereal disease, diseases afflicting the throat.

Waiting for someone: Will come bringing good news.

Looking for someone: Will soon return on his own or his whereabouts will become known. Look to the southeast or east.

Lost article: Can be found. Search in the southeast or east.

Travel: Propitious.

Lawsuit and disputes: Victory.

Employment: A good job can be found.

Examination: Excellent scores.

New business, change of occupation or specialization, and moving: Propitious.

Weather: Cloudy, later clearing.

HEXAGRAM 43

KUAI

guai

Break through (Resoluteness)

Primary	Upper	Tui	Joyous
	Lower	Chien	Creative
Nuclear	Above	Chien	Creative
	Below	Chien	Creative

Kuai means awkwardness, deviation, estrangement. In this hexagram one *yin* or broken line sits atop five *yang* or solid lines. It cannot have intercourse with *yang* and is but waiting to be replaced or superseded by the *yang* force. With the five *yang* lines underneath, the one *yin* with which they cannot have intercourse make the situation awkward. From another viewpoint, the *yang* force is flourishing. Soon it will be excessively strong, enough so as to cause problems. It is the catastrophe that follows a mounting of tension. In divining, it means that overzealousness can cause awkward situations and suggests a highly dangerous situation that can be saved only through unwavering resoluteness.

THE FORTUNE

Though fortunes are prosperous, soon trouble and hardship will appear. Be cautious, self-disciplined and earnestly keep to the correct way. You may get into a quarrel or fall sick from overwork. You may also mishandle documents or contracts and thus suffer a loss. A subordinate may secretly cause you trouble. Flooding is a possibility.

Wish: The influence of emotion may cause failure. But with caution success is possible.

Marriage: Not a good match and cannot be successful. Even if the marriage goes through, the couple will break up later.

Love: One-sided. One side is trying too hard. Take a step back and pause a moment for self-reflection. Impetuousness and eagerness will be of no use. Failure is a distinct possibility.

Family: For the present the family fortunes are flourishing. But there is a possibility that they will decline later.

Children: More boys than girls. At first good fortune but later adversity. Pregnancy: boy; possibly a difficult birth.

Capital loan: Success will be very difficult.

Business: Failure and loss possible.

Stock market: Prices high but will drop suddenly later.

Life span: Basically healthy, but you may encounter the unfortunate because of improper care of your body or some unexpected calamity.

Sickness: Serious and dangerous but as you are basically of strong constitution an operation or some kind of special treatment will enable you to recover. Afflictions of the head and kidney regions. Peritonitis or malignant tumors.

Waiting for someone: Will not come.

Looking for someone: Far away, whereabouts unknown. This person may even be in danger. Look with speed and urgency near some water to the west or northwest.

Lost article: Lost outside, unrecoverable.

Travel: Misfortunes and obstacles en route. Reconsider your plans.

Lawsuit and disputes: Defeat probable; best to desist.

Employment: Difficult.

Examination: Very poor scores.

New business, change of occupation or specialization, and moving: Unfavorable.

Weather: Rainy.

HEXAGRAM 44

KOU

gou

Coming to meet

Primary	Upper	Chien	Creative
	Lower	Sun	Gentle
Nuclear	Above	Chien	Creative
	Below	Chien	Creative

Kou means intercourse, coming in contact with, pairing off, and meeting. The bottom line is *yin*, or broken, situated below five solid *yang* lines. *Ch'ien* (Hexagram 1: the Creative) is composed of six solid or *yang* lines. The extreme nature of the *yang* force brings into existence the *yin* force. Hence, Hexagram 44 is derived from Hexagram 1. The existence of one *yin* line below the five *yang* lines means that intercourse between the two forces has begun. The image is of a girl who offers herself to men and suggests that action should not be taken merely for the sake of influence. The *yin* force is on the rise and the *yang* is declining. Beware of unexpected encounters, accidents, or misfortunes. This hexagram suggests the beginning of a decline in fortunes.

THE FORTUNE

Fortunes changing for the worse. Be careful and on your guard to prevent the beginning of declining fortunes. You may encounter misfortune, someone may harm or slander you, and a woman may cause you trouble and loss.

Wish: Unexpected obstacles will lead to failure.

Marriage: An ill match; best reconsider.

Love: The other party is not sincere.

Family: Caution is advised as the family fortunes are beginning to decline.

Children: Improper behavior by children will cause trouble and woe for the parents. Pay close attention to the education and training of your children. Pregnancy: girl.

Capital loan: Not easily achieved. Seek the help of a woman and success may be possible.

Business: Loss and failure are possible. But businesses that deal with women—perfume, flowers, cosmetics, and the like—will prosper.

Stock market: Prices will go down from now.

Life span: Naturally healthy. The curse of disease may afflict you, making it difficult to keep your good health. Take care of your body.

Sickness: Condition worsening. Careful convalescence is needed. Venereal disease, tuberculosis, and hemorrhoids.

Waiting for someone: If it is a woman, she will come. If it is a man, he will run into some obstacles en route and not come.

Looking for someone: Sexual complications will make the search lengthy. But this person is safe and sound. He may return on his own or his whereabouts may become known. Look to the west or northwest.

Lost article: Might be found in some unexpected place. Search in the west or northwest.

Travel: An auspicious meeting along the way, especially for women.

Lawsuit and disputes: Lengthy, time-consuming, and unfavorable.

Employment: Unsuccessful. Seeking the help of a woman may lead to success.

Examination: Poor score.

New business, change of occupation or specialization, and moving: Unfavorable. Obstacles will prevent realization.

Weather: Fine weather for the moment but will worsen beginning now.

HEXAGRAM 45

TS'UI

cui

Gathering together (Massing)

Primary	Upper	Tui	Joyous
	Lower	K'un	Receptive
Nuclear	Above	Sun	Gentle
	Below	Ken	Keeping Still

Ts'ui means to gather, assemble, or come together. The lower trigram *K'un* stands for the multitude and for obedience or submission and following.

The upper trigram *Tui* stands for happiness and pleasure. Together it means that the multitudes are happy and in compliance. Line five, counting from the bottom, is the ruler's line and line four is the chief minister's line. Both are *yang*. The other four *yin* or broken lines surround the two *yang* lines and obey them. In divining, it means that one's spirits and financial resources are gathered together. It is a very auspicious hexagram.

THE FORTUNE

The gathering of prosperity. Others may render cooperation and large profits may be realized. Best to follow the advice of one's seniors. Rich farm harvest.

Wish: Can be realized.

Marriage: Happy, well-suited match. Smooth success.

Love: Success—each treating the other with the respect afforded a guest.

Family: Family members share in happiness and joy. Fortunes flourishing.

Children: Many, existing in harmony. Pregnancy: girl.

Capital loan: Can be realized.

Business: Flourishing business, smooth profits.

Stock market: Gradual rise in prices.

Life span: Healthy long life.

Sickness: Quick recovery. Afflictions of the chest and abdominal regions.

Waiting for someone: Will come bringing something nice.

Looking for someone: Do not worry. He will soon return voluntarily or his whereabouts will become known. Look in the west or southwest.

Lost article: Can be found. Search in the west or southwest.

Travel: Travel will be beneficial.

Lawsuit and disputes: Contention is unfavorable. Best to seek a compromise.

Employment: Can be found without trouble.

Examination: Good score.

New business, change of occupation or specialization, and moving: Proceed.

Weather: Heavy rains, perhaps even flooding.

H E X A G R A M   4 6

SHENG

sheng

Pushing upward

Primary	*Upper*	*K'un*	*Receptive*
	Lower	*Sun*	*Gentle*
Nuclear	*Above*	*Chen*	*Arousing*
	Below	*Tui*	*Joyous*

Sheng means to rise, ascend, move forward, and advance. The upper trigram is *K'un*, symbolizing the earth, while the lower trigram *Sun* symbolizes trees. The hexagram then looks like the seeds of trees pushing upward, ready to break out from the earth, gradually growing into tall trees. Trees grow slowly so the upward movement of this hexagram is slow and regular like going up stairs, not a fast jump upward. When the seedling grows it absorbs elements from its environment—fertilizer from the soil and rain and sunshine. It is passive. In the same manner, be yielding and bide your time. Be diligent and your ability and talents will be recognized. In divining, it means that this is the time your talents and resources are developing in the correct manner.

THE FORTUNE

Things are going as hoped. It is the time for gradual forward progress. It is auspicious for things to be done in a logical and well-planned order. Do not act rashly or impetuously. Developments to the south are auspicious. It is beneficial to follow the powerful, influential, and virtuous. You might rise in rank or position or have your salary raised. Pregnancy is possible for brides.

Wish: Definite realization. Best to rely on the help of someone powerful or influential.

Marriage: Good match with brilliant future.

Love: Success possible but do not rush.

Family: Gradual flourishing of family fortunes.

Children: Good fortune; children appear likely to succeed. Pregnancy: girl.

Capital loan: Success definite.

Business: Profits as hoped but do not act rashly.

Stock market: Gradual rise in prices.

Life span: Healthy and long life.

Sickness: Recovery will take some time, but in the end recovery is possible. Afflictions of the internal organs, especially the lower abdominal region.

Waiting for someone: Will come late.

Looking for someone: The search will take time but this person is safe and sound and can be found. Search in the southwest and the southeast.

Lost article: Can be found. Search to the southeast or southwest.

Travel: Propitious.

Lawsuit and disputes: Victory or a very beneficial settlement.

Employment: Your goal can be realized.

Examination: Excellent score.

New business, change of occupation or specialization, and moving: Proceed.

Weather: Warm, genial weather with nice breezes, lasting for quite a while.

K'UN

kun

Oppression (Exhaustion)

	Primary	Upper	Tui	Joyous
		Lower	K'an	Abysmal
	Nuclear	Above	Sun	Gentle
		Below	Li	Clinging

K'un means difficulty, adversity, suffering, distress, misery, and fatigue. The upper trigram is *Tui* symbolizing marshes and the lower trigram is *K'an* symbolizing water. Water normally collects in marshes, but in this hexagram the water is below the marsh, meaning that the water has leaked out, drying the marsh. Things of necessity are not around. The situation is dangerous. In divining, it means that one is in the midst of difficulty and deficiency. By keeping to the way of integrity at all times, however, one can with self-discipline and patience wait for fortunes to change.

THE FORTUNE

A time of hardship, distress, failure, and solitariness. Advancement will lead to adversity. Best to retreat and maintain a position. Wait for fortunes to change with forbearance and self-discipline.

Wish: Cannot be realized.

Marriage: Distressing, ill-suited match. Will not succeed. Best look for someone else.

Love: Will end in failure.

Family: Declining fortunes, financial difficulties. You must work hard and struggle to open up the family fortunes. In the end you will succeed in reaping the fruits of well-being.

Children: No children or distress caused by children. Pregnancy: girl.

Capital loan: Will not succeed.

Business: Many obstacles; business will not go as hoped.

Stock market: Low prices, will drop even lower.

Life span: Unhealthy and weak. A short life if strict self-discipline is not imposed.

Sickness: Serious illness, lengthy and protracted. Hope for recovery lies in increased convalescent techniques. Lung ailments and diseases affecting the internal organs of the chest and abdominal regions.

Waiting for someone: Will not come. There is a chance this person may come after a long time has elapsed.

Looking for someone: Whereabouts unknown. There is nothing to do but wait for events to develop naturally. News may thus come naturally.

Lost article: Not easily found. Search in the north or west.

Travel: Unfavorable.

Lawsuit and disputes: Time-consuming and vexing. Best to drop it or let the case be settled naturally.

Employment: No hope.

Examination: Low score.

New business, change of occupation or specialization, and moving: Not the right time.

Weather: Continuing bad weather.

CHING

jing

The well

	Primary	Upper	*K'an*	*Abysmal*
		Lower	*Sun*	*Gentle*
	Nuclear	Above	*Li*	*Clinging*
		Below	*Tui*	*Joyous*

Ching means a well for storing water. The upper trigram *K'an* symbolizes water while the lower trigram *Sun* symbolizes wood. It also has the meaning of entering or coming and going. Taken as a whole the hexagram gives the picture of a wooden bucket removing water from a well. Ancient tribal cultures were built next to running water or surrounding a well. Wells allow mankind to draw water without exhausting the supply. Yet man must implement effective measures to enjoy the blessings of a well and have a source to quench his thirst. In divination, this hexagram means that one ought to do good deeds to benefit others. At the same time one should remain calm and peaceful like a well.

THE FORTUNE

Quiet and calm fortune. Best to avoid a positive course of action. Maintain your present position in order to maintain peace, tranquility, and a trouble-free situation.

Wish: No hope for the moment. With persevering diligence success may come.

Marriage: Sound, good match. Overzealousness or hurry will lead to defeat. Sincerity, patience, and diligence will lead to success.

Love: Go naturally, treating the other party with sincerity, and success will come. Do not be too eager.

Family: Harmonious, calm, peaceful.

Children: Fine and happy children who enjoy well-being. Pregnancy: boy. Safe and smooth delivery.

Capital loan: No hope for the moment.

Business: Profit will come through restrained, regulated advancement. Do not act rashly. Move instead with honesty and dedication.

Stock market: Prices falling.

Life span: Healthy, long life.

Sickness: Recovery through patient convalescence. Colds, afflictions of the urinary organs; afflictions in the lower half of the body.

Waiting for someone: Will not come for the moment. Wait patiently.

Looking for someone: Hiding nearby, but the search will consume much time. However, this person is safe and sound and can be found after some time. Search in the north or southeast.

Lost article: Lost indoors. Patient searching can lead to success. Search in low-lying places in the southeast.

Travel: For the moment, it is best to wait.

Lawsuit and disputes: Unfavorable. Best to seek a compromise.

Employment: Do not be impetuous or excited.

Examination: Average score.

New business, change of occupation or specialization, and moving: Best to maintain present circumstances.

Weather: Cloudy with occasional rain.

KO

ge

Revolution (Molting)

Primary	Upper	Tui	Joyous
	Lower	Li	Clinging
Nuclear	Above	Chien	Creative
	Below	Sun	Gentle

Ko means revolution, change, reform, and renovation. The upper trigram *Tui* symbolizes marshes and the lower trigram *Li* symbolizes fire. The fire is in the marsh. If it burns fiercely, then the water of the marsh will dry. If the water is greater, then the fire will be extinguished. Hence the hexagram pictures reform or change. *Li* also represents the sun. Here it is setting in the west, which is represented by *Tui*. Thus the hexagram has the meaning of change from day to night. Moreover, *Li* stands for summer and *Tui* for autumn. Hence the hexagram also connotes seasonal or weather changes. *Ko* is the process of shifting old things to the new. This renovation should follow the correct road of change. In divination, it means that both personal matters and those of one's surroundings have reached a period of change.

THE FORTUNE

A time when all things may change. You should with courage and wisdom put various matters in order, making new arrangements. If this is done the fortune will be fresh, and bright prospects will appear. Nonetheless, the most important thing is to keep to the correct path. You may possibly change your place of residence or even become involved in complications.

Wish: At first difficulties, but success will come later. Best to proceed with a new course of action.

Marriage: Success possible. First marriages are unfavorable. The husband and wife will later separate. Remarriages are propitious.

Love: Unfavorable. Must change tactics or find someone new.

Family: Complications and hardships. You must have the courage and determination to engage in the renovation of family affairs. At first there will be drudgery, toil, and hardship but eventually you will reap happiness and well-being.

Children: A dilemma or contradiction exists between parents and children. You must devise a way to reverse this adverse situation. Pregnancy: girl.

Capital loan: Difficulties. Change your methods and proceed; success will then be possible.

Business: Change your course of action, and success and profits will possibly be yours.

Stock market: Fluctuating, unstable prices. Will rise later.

Life span: Weak and sickly when young. After reaching maturity, your strength will gradually increase and a healthy, long life can be yours.

Sickness: Life in danger. A slight hope exists if you change doctors, the hospital, or method of treatment. Heart ailments, eye diseases, and afflictions of the lower abdomen.

Waiting for someone: Will not come. If he should come, he will have been forced to do so.

Looking for someone: You must change the method of searching in order to find this person. Look in the west or south.

Lost article: It has already changed owners. Not easily recoverable.

Travel: To go out is auspicious. But be careful during the journey.

Lawsuit and disputes: Change tactics and victory is a possibility.

Employment: Change tactics or method of search and you will have success.

Examination: Fairly good score, but not ideal.

New business, change of occupation or specialization, and moving: Propitious.

Weather: Changing weather conditions. Clear weather will change to rainy and rainy to clear and so on.

HEXAGRAM 50

TING

ding

The caldron

Primary	*Upper*	*Li*	*Clinging*
	Lower	*Sun*	*Gentle*
Nuclear	*Above*	*Tui*	*Joyous*
	Below	*Chien*	*Creative*

Ting refers to a sacrificial or ritual vessel or caldron which has two ears and three legs. Looking at the shape of the hexagram, we can see it resembles the *Ting* tripod. The bottom line is broken (*yin*) and represents the legs. Lines two, three, and four are solid or *yang* and represent the body of the pot. The broken line five resembles the two ears of the pot, and the top solid line represents a cover.

The upper trigram is *Li* which symbolizes fire. The lower trigram is *Sun* which symbolizes wood. Taken as a whole, the hexagram pictures a wood fire cooking food. The three legs of the *Ting* tripod stand for the environment, wealth, and intelligence—all three being in a secure and sound condition. It means that all things are complete and in order, secure, and in fixed positions. In divination, this hexagram means stability and unobstructed flow.

THE FORTUNE

Secure, abundant, and unhindered fortune. A superior may take an interest in you and bring your talents into full play. Cooperative ventures are auspicious.

Wish: Will realize goal.

Marriage: Fortunate, flourishing good match. Success definite. A third person may appear—a lover, a mother-in-law, or someone—yet the marriage will have a harmonious and satisfactory outcome.

Love: Definite success.

Family: Fortunes already prosperous and will become even more flourishing.

Children: Children blessed with outstanding talent. They will be successful in the future. Pregnancy: girl.

Capital loan: Success.

Business: Great profits.

Stock market: Stable and favorable.

Life span: Healthy, long life.

Sickness: Recovery soon. Diseases of the digestive organs, diabetes.

Waiting for someone: Will come.

Looking for someone: This person will be found soon or will soon return on his own free will. Look in the southeast or south.

Lost article: Can be found. Search in the southeast or south.

Travel: Greatly propitious.

Lawsuit and disputes: Victory.

Employment: Smooth going.

Examination: Excellent score.

New business, change of occupation or specialization, and moving: Greatly propitious.

Weather: Clear fine weather with a gentle breeze.

CHEN

zhen

The arousing (Shock, thunder)

	Primary	Upper	Chen	Arousing
		Lower	Chen	Arousing
	Nuclear	Above	K'an	Abysmal
		Below	Ken	Keeping Still

Chen means to excite, inspire, stir, shock, and arouse. Both upper and lower trigrams are *Chen*. In this hexagram the two solid *yang* lines, the bottom line of each trigram, are repressed by the broken *yin* lines. Suppressed as it is, the *yang* force's wrath is aroused. With determination the *yang* force is striving to break through the suppression of the *yin* and expand. The trigram *Chen* stands for thunder. Since both trigrams are *Chen*, the picture is of thunder everywhere, rousing and moving. In divination, it means that it is now the time to become aroused, to overcome difficulties, and to fulfill desires or ambitions.

THE FORTUNE

Although there are many difficulties, the fortune is changing from the dark to the light. Carefully conduct affairs, proceeding step by step in logical order, and overcome the difficulties. Your goals can then be reached and good fortune is yours. You may enjoy sudden fame or fortune or receive the trust and support of the multitude. You may succeed in or inherit someone's business and reap both fame and fortune. On the other hand, over self-confidence, rejection of the opinions of others, or short-sightedness may lead to conflict or failure. You must be careful.

Wish: You can eliminate difficulties and reap success.

Marriage: First marriages are unfortunate. Remarriages are propitious.

Love: Though there may be some rough waves, success will be realized in the end.

Family: Hardships, trouble, and difficulties. With aroused determination you may reap flourishing family fortunes and happiness.

Children: The children will cause you distress and trouble. But the children are all able to strive and each realizes happiness and success. As the children are stubborn and willful, special care must be taken in their upbringing, centering on training and guidance. Pregnancy: boy.

Capital loan: At first many difficulties exist that must be overcome. Once they are overcome success is yours.

Business: Once troubles are broken through, great profits are yours.

Stock market: Prices rising.

Life span: Healthy, long life.

Sickness: Serious with gradual recovery. Nervous disorders, neuralgia, brain diseases, and acute internal disorders.

Waiting for someone: Will come unexpectedly early.

Looking for someone: Far away. Something frightening, but no real danger. Look in the east.

Lost article: Search with utmost speed, for if it is not found soon, you will not get it back. Search in the east.

Travel: Trouble is a possibility midway, but you will realize the purpose of your trip.

Lawsuit and disputes: Handle all with a firm and strong attitude and a favorable outcome will be yours.

Employment: Difficulties. Strength can overcome them and you can reach your goal.

Examination: Anxiety, but your score is good.

New business, change of occupation or specialization, and moving: Proceed, but do not force it.

Weather: Unstable, possible thunder showers.

HEXAGRAM 52

KEN

gen

Keeping still, mountain

Primary	Upper	Ken	Keeping Still
	Lower	Ken	Keeping Still
Nuclear	Above	Chen	Arousing
	Below	Kan	Abysmal

Ken means motionlessness, rest, stoppage, and silence. Both upper and lower trigrams are *Ken*, which symbolizes mountains. The picture is of mountains sitting still and unmoving. In divination, it means that like the mountains one ought to be still and unmoving, waiting for the right moment to come.

THE FORTUNE

Many obstructions. Fortune stagnant and unmoving. Be indifferent to worldly gains, do not talk too much, be noble and exalted like a mountain, and maintain unshakable beliefs or convictions and wait for the opportune moment.

Wish: Unsuccessful. You must wait.

Marriage: Incompatible, bad match. Moreover, success is not possible.

Love: One-sided; unsuccessful.

Family: Fortunes at a standstill. The family is at odds, much distress. Only patient, hard work can overcome the difficulties and bring about happiness and well-being.

Children: Strong personalities, very independent. They resemble the father more than the mother. Pregnancy: boy. Possibility of a difficult delivery.

Capital loan: Will not succeed. You must wait.

Business: Stagnant, no great gains or losses, but many headaches.

Stock market: Very little movement.

Life span: Trouble-ridden health, possibility of a short life. You must pay attention to self-discipline.

Sickness: Protracted. Tuberculosis, hardening of the arteries, and brain diseases.

Waiting for someone: Will not come.

Looking for someone: This person may be back in his original place. Look in a high place in the northeast.

Lost article: Not easily found. Search in the northeast.

Travel: Unfavorable. Wait and see later.

Lawsuit and disputes: Time-consuming and unfavorable. Best to seek a compromise.

Employment: Time-consuming without any real result. You must wait.

Examination: Either an average or bad score.

New business, change of occupation or specialization, and moving: Unfavorable. Better maintain your present situation.

Weather: Cloudy.

CHIEN

jian

Development (Gradual progress)

Primary	Upper	Sun	Gentle
	Lower	Ken	Keeping Still
Nuclear	Above	Li	Clinging
	Below	K'an	Abysmal

Chien means orderly, gradual advancement or progress. The upper trigram *Sun* stands for trees while the lower trigram *Ken* symbolizes mountains. Taken as a whole the hexagram is a picture of trees growing on a mountain. Trees grow slowly and gradually, thus the hexagram suggests gradual advancement. In divination, it means that everything is gradually opening up. In the *I-Ching* the water fowl flies from water to land to trees to mountains. The same is true for women who go to strange places to marry. Movement in both cases brings well-being and happiness.

THE FORTUNE

Fortunes gradually opening up; everything is gradually becoming smooth. The future is full of brightness and hope. Success will come from gradual advancement. To forge ahead too quickly or impetuously is unfavorable. There is a possibility of a trip by air. For women, this hexagram means the possibility of some joyful event occurring.

Wish: Will not be realized immediately. A period of time must elapse before the wish is realized.

Marriage: A good match. Success is possible.

Love: Success is possible. But you must proceed slowly. Rashness or impetuousness will lead to failure.

Family: Gradual expansion of the family fortunes and the attaining of blessings and happiness. To leave the family and make a living on the outside can result in considerable accomplishment.

Children: Obedient and honest. They all have good prospects. The older you

become, the more your children will bring you happiness. Pregnancy: girl.

Capital loan: Cannot be realized immediately. A certain period of time will have to elapse.

Business: Gradual success and profits. Do not be hurried or rash.

Stock market: Gradually rising.

Life span: Healthy, long life.

Sickness: Recovery will be time-consuming. Care in convalescence will mean recovery. Diseases of the ears, nose, stomach, and bowels.

Waiting for someone: Will come a little later, but this person will definitely come.

Looking for someone: Far away; the search will be time-consuming. But this person is safe and sound, and in the end his whereabouts will become known. Look in the northeast or southeast.

Lost article: The search will be time-consuming, but the article can be found. Search patiently to the southeast or northeast, in high places.

Travel: Propitious.

Lawsuit and disputes: Continuous stubborn contention will be unfavorable. Best to decide on a course of compromise and proceed with patience.

Employment: It will take some time but in the end you will be able to find a good job.

Examination: Gradual improvement in scores.

New business, change of occupation or specialization, and moving: Proceed; auspicious. But do not be overanxious or rash.

Weather: Gradually turning better.

HEXAGRAM 54

KUEI MEI

gui mei

The marrying maiden

Primary	Upper	Chen	Arousing
	Lower	Tui	Joyous
Nuclear	Above	K'an	Abysmal
	Below	Li	Clinging

Kuei Mei means that the younger sister marries before the elder sister. In ancient China this violated social conventions and was regarded as being improper. The upper trigram *Chen* stands for the eldest son while the lower trigram *Tui* represents the youngest daughter and joy or delight. The union of a younger woman and older man based on the urgings of passion was also regarded as violating the ethical code. In divination, this hexagram represents the violation of social conventions or ethical codes and actions based on emotions. As such, unexpected misfortune is not easily avoided. One must be careful as a result.

THE FORTUNE

Infatuated with physical pleasures that violate social conventions, you will soon encounter misfortune. Thus you must turn over a new leaf and reform yourself in order to avoid calamity. Nothing will remain consistent from the start to the very end. You may also become involved in some complications. For women who are engaged in the business of night life—barmaids, dance-hall girls, cabaret girls, and so on—you will find a good patron.

Wish: At first smooth success will seem likely, but it will end in failure.

Marriage: Though already intimate, the success of the marriage appears unlikely. Even if the marriage takes place, this is not a harmonious match. For women, you may be the second wife or even mistress.

Love: Not suited for each other. Though there may be a period of tender affection, it will end sadly in separation.

Family: From outward appearances the family seems to be prosperous and harmonious. In reality, however, there is disunion, disharmony, and unhappiness; the family fortunes are declining.

Children: Debauched, dissipated, or wild. Questionable moral character, especially for daughters. Pregnancy: girl.

Capital loan: Unsuccessful.

Business: At first things will appear to be going smoothly and well. In fact, miscalculations and errors in planning will summon the unfavorable—loss or failure.

Stock market: In the midst of falling prices.

Life span: Heretofore healthy, but improper care of the body and disregard of cleanliness will lead to physical harm.

Sickness: Recoverable. However, continued neglect of the care of your body and disregard of cleanliness will make the situation worse, even to the point of hopelessness. Venereal disease, liver or chest ailments.

Waiting for someone: Will not come.

Looking for someone: Has gone away because of disharmony in the home or some sexual affair. This person may be in danger. Search in the east or west. This person might not be found.

Lost article: Unrecoverable.

Travel: Obstacles and misfortunes. Best to cancel plans.

Lawsuit and disputes: Unreasonable contention will definitely lead to defeat. Best to compromise.

Employment: No result.

Examination: Low score.

New business, change of occupation or specialization, and moving: Adverse. Best to stop for the moment.

Weather: Cloudy, later clearing.

FENG

feng

Abundance (Fullness)

	Primary	Upper	Chen	Arousing
		Lower	Li	Clinging
	Nuclear	Above	Tui	Joyous
		Below	Sun	Gentle

Feng means abundance, plentifulness, and prosperity. The upper trigram *Chen* stands for movement while the lower trigram *Li* symbolizes brilliance or light. The hexagram, then, depicts honest and open movement. Honest and open advancement in all things will lead to success and development. Once success is realized plentifulness and abundance will follow. *Chen* also stands for the imposing, prestige, and courage, and *Li* stands for wisdom and intelligence. Together, wisdom and the awe-inspiring have no equal in magnificence. In divination, it means that exceptional prosperity is at hand. Since everything declines after reaching a peak, you must devise a course of action to guard against this decline.

THE FORTUNE

Enjoying smooth, good fortune. However, complacency, neglect, and relaxed efforts will lead to a decline in your fortune. At the same time you have the luck of being able to earn a great sum of money. But avoid being extravagant, wasteful, and vain. The possibility exists that being too much in the spotlight will lead to being cheated or involvement in some trouble. For those involved in the arts and in cultural endeavors, a future of unlimited prospects.

Wish: Smooth realization of goal.

Marriage: Flourishing, good match.

Love: Success possible; but selfish actions without regard for the other can spell failure.

Family: Flourishing prosperity. Nevertheless, arrogance or haughty behavior can lead to a decline.

Children: Much happiness and well-being for them. Nonetheless, you must not be remiss in their upbringing. Pregnancy: boy.

Capital loan: Success.

Business: Great profits possible.

Stock market: Prices rising.

Life span: Healthy, long life.

Sickness: Serious. Your health has heretofore not been very strong so special care must be taken in convalescence in order to assure recovery. Diseases afflicting the nervous system, the stomach, the bowels, and diabetes.

Waiting for someone: Will come bringing good tidings.

Looking for someone: Do not worry. Whereabouts will become known soon or this person will return voluntarily.

Lost article: Carelessness caused the loss. Search calmly and with a composed mind and you will find it. Search to the east or south.

Travel: Propitious.

Lawsuit and disputes: Victory or a favorable settlement or compromise.

Employment: You can find a good job or position.

Examination: Excellent scores.

New business, change of occupation or specialization, and moving: Auspicious. Proceed.

Weather: Good weather at the moment but it can change to bad weather.

LÜ

lü

The wanderer

Primary	Upper	Li	Clinging
	Lower	Ken	Keeping Still
Nuclear	Above	Tui	Joyous
	Below	Sun	Gentle

Lü means travel, journey, or the traveler. The upper trigram *Li* symbolizes fire while the lower trigram *Ken* symbolizes mountains. Taken together the hexagram depicts a fire burning in the wilds of a mountain. A mountain is stationary and unmoving. But the fire is burning from one place to another, continually moving. In this case the mountain stands for the journey and the fire for the traveler, who is shifting and unstable. In divination, it is like someone who is out wandering away from home. In all matters this person feels unnatural, unfamiliar, lonely, and uneasy. The appearance is of toil and labor.

THE FORTUNE

Like on a trip, the fortune lacks stability. Floating, drifting, and unstable in life, all things do not go according to hopes. Prudence and self-restraint are called for. Do not rush things or act too positively. Handle matters with a gentle, amiable attitude. If these things are done, then the situation will settle down. The following may occur: a change in your work, job, or occupation may leave you alone and without assistance; while on a journey some trouble or complications may arise at home; changing your place of residence may lead to trouble and bother; you may even face the misfortune of a fire.

Wish: Small wishes can be realized, but there is no hope for large ones.

Marriage: The emotions on both sides are not completely compatible or of one accord. This and other problems make marriage unsuccessful. Even if the marriage should go through, the couple will suffer many difficulties and problems. An unstable, ill-suited match.

Love: The intentions of the other party are not fixed. This will lead to failure.

Family: No feelings among flesh and blood. The family fortunes are unstable and unfavorable.

Children: Feelings between parents and children are not in harmony. Lonely, unlucky, and unfortunate. Pregnancy: girl.

Capital loans: Can borrow only a small amount.

Business: Neither great profits nor great losses. Business is just so-so.

Stock market: Unstable prices. Will rise later.

Life span: Weak and unhealthy. A short life is a possibility.

Sickness: Uncertain, changeable, unstable condition. Protracted and time-consuming. Life in danger. Diseases afflicting the respiratory and digestive organs.

Waiting for someone: May come after a considerable number of days. However, the chance this person will not come is great.

Looking for someone: Far away and staying in an uncertain place. Whereabouts not easily discovered.

Lost article: It has already fallen into someone else's hands and cannot be recovered.

Travel: Although trouble and obstacles will impede the journey, the unfortunate fact is that you must make the journey.

Lawsuit and disputes: Time-consuming and in vain. Best to give it up.

Employment: No hope at least for the moment.

Examination: Poor score.

New business, change of occupation or specialization, and moving: Adverse. Best to wait.

Weather: Unstable, bad weather.

HEXAGRAM 57

SUN

sun

The gentle (The penetrating, wind)

Primary	*Upper*	*Sun*	*Gentle*
	Lower	*Sun*	*Gentle*
Nuclear	*Above*	*Li*	*Clinging*
	Below	*Tui*	*Joyous*

Both the upper and lower trigrams are *Sun* and symbolize the wind. The wind enters everywhere and gives the hexagram the meaning of to come and go. In terms of shape, the broken *yin* line in each trigram is submerged below two solid *yang* lines. The *yin* force recedes or withdraws downward in a negative manner; but in this case, submerged as it is below the *yang* lines, it has no place to retreat to. Thus, this hexagram also means obedience and compliance. In divination, it means that one cannot take action as the principal mover, leader, or director. Instead one must move as if going with the wind, following the lead of others, letting the situation develop on its own. In this way advantage can be had.

THE FORTUNE

The fortune is moving like the wind, unstable and wandering. In handling affairs or dealing with people take a humble, submissive attitude and adapt to changing circumstances quickly. If this is done then you may reap slight rewards. You may encounter the following misfortunes: robbery, disadvantage stemming from hesitancy and indecision, and loss or failure caused by conflict or impulsive actions.

Wish: A reasonable wish within your sphere can be realized. Excessive wishes cannot be realized.

Marriage: Chance for success is small. There is a third person involved and the other party cannot decide which one to marry.

Love: Waves. Handle the situation with calm and composed determination and success can be had.

Family: Many obstacles and complications. Follow the advice of your elders and remain calm and quiet and the family fortunes can begin to flourish.

Children: Difficult to avoid toil and distress in bringing up the children. Nevertheless, the children are obedient and loyal. Pregnancy: girl.

Capital loan: Only a small amount can be borrowed.

Business: Small profits possible.

Stock market: Prices unstable at the moment but will rise later.

Life span: Difficult to avoid obstructions to your health, but with proper care of the body you can attain a long life.

Sickness: Condition will change and fluctuate. Lengthy and protracted; but there is no danger to your life. Disorders of the nervous system, such as neuralgia; venereal disease and diabetes.

Waiting for someone: Will come very late.

Looking for someone: This person feels he has been made a fool of and has gone away to the southwest. This person will return, however, from the southeast.

Lost article: This article is perhaps buried or placed under something. Look in the southeast.

Travel: The journey may take more time than necessary, but the journey is possible.

Lawsuit and disputes: Obstacles and troubles are many. The best method for gaining advantage would be to entrust the task of mediation to someone with power or authority.

Employment: Time-consuming and you will not find ideal work.

Examination: Average score.

New business, change of occupation or specialization, and moving: You may proceed, but do not act impulsively and do not force the situation.

Weather: Sunny and clear; strong winds.

HEXAGRAM 58

TUI

dui

The joyous, lake

Primary	Upper	Tui	Joyous
	Lower	Tui	Joyous
Nuclear	Above	Sun	Gentle
	Below	Li	Clinging

Tui means joy or pleasure. Both trigrams of the hexagram are *Tui*. In each one a broken line or *yin* sits in a commanding position atop two solid or *yang* lines. The *yang* force represents firmness and nobility while the *yin* force represents meekness and humility. For the meek and humble line to be respected and in a position superior to the two strong and noble lines is, of course, a cause for happiness and joy. *Tui* stands for marshes. Marshes moisten and enrich myriad things, causing them delight and joy. Since both of the trigrams of this hexagram are *Tui* the ideas of enrichment and joy are doubled. In divination, it means that you are in the midst of joyful and delightful good fortune.

THE FORTUNE

Generally speaking, an auspicious fortune with everything going as hoped. You may experience a happy event. On the other hand, careless words may lead to trouble or a woman may cause you distress or anguish. In treating people, be gentle, mild, and sincere. In handling affairs be cautious and prudent. If these things are done the good fortune can be maintained.

Wish: Smooth success.

Marriage: Two women contending for the same man—quarrels and fights. Success is not easy. Remarriages are fortunate.

Love: Quarrels. But success is possible if both parties respect each other.

Family: Harmonious, happy, and blessed with well-being. However, there is a possibility that the husband and wife frequently quarrel and fight. Both sides should be tolerant and more yielding.

Children: Harmonious relationship between parents and children. But the parents must not spoil the children. Pregnancy: girl.

Capital loan: Success.

Business: Profits. But guard against setbacks on the way.

Stock market: Rising prices.

Life span: A healthy, long life.

Sickness: Recovery definite. But do not be too self-satisfied. Venereal disease, lung ailments such as tuberculosis, and afflictions of the stomach and bowels.

Waiting for someone: Will come bringing good will.

Looking for someone: Something to do with sex. This person can be found in the not distant future.

Lost article: Can be found. Search in the west.

Travel: Propitious.

Lawsuit and disputes: Advantageous to seek a compromise.

Employment: Goal can be realized.

Examination: Good score.

New business, change of occupation or specialization, and moving: Propitious.

Weather: Rainy.

HUAN

huan

Dispersion (Dissolution)

	Primary	Upper	Sun	Gentle
		Lower	K'an	Abysmal
	Nuclear	Above	Ken	Keeping Still
		Below	Chen	Arousing

Huan means dispersal, scattering, and dissolution. The upper trigram *Sun* symbolizes the wind and the lower trigram *K'an* the water. When the wind blows, the water is scattered. *K'an* also represents winter and ice while *Sun* represents spring and wind. The hexagram thus depicts the spring winds dispersing the bitter cold and ice of winter. In divination, it means that the bad fortune of trouble and hardship is beginning to disperse—the start of expansion and development.

THE FORTUNE

Fortunes are beginning to change and hardships to abate. But do not be too much at ease. Failure will come from being heedless, imprudent, and too free. Great good fortune for business involving ships and for the moving or shipping business. The following things may occur: a journey away from home, gaining the assistance of someone, or failure through lack of willpower or fickleness.

Wish: Determine a course of action, stick with it all the way and success can be realized.

Marriage: Obstacles can be cleared and success realized. In the marriage, early hardships and toil cannot be easily avoided. Happiness and well-being will come later.

Love: Obstruction at first is not easily avoided. Proceed with an unswerving, unbendable spirit and success can be had.

Family: Toil and hardship at first, then a gradual change in fortunes.

Children: Trouble and toil because of the children in the beginning. Happiness and well-being later on. Pregnancy: girl. Safe delivery.

Capital loan: Though there are difficulties, success is possible.

Business: Small profits possible.

Stock market: Sudden drop in prices.

Life span: Many illnesses while young but after maturity good health and a long life can be had.

Sickness: A moment of danger, but recovery in the end. Affected areas:

blood system and respiratory organs.

Waiting for someone: Will either come earlier than expected or will never come.

Looking for someone: Far away. It will not be easy to locate this person.

Lost article: Lost on the outside and cannot be recovered.

Travel: Proceed.

Lawsuit and disputes: Harm to both parties. Best to compromise.

Employment: Will go according to hopes.

Examination: Good score.

New business, change of occupation or specialization, and moving: Propitious.

Weather: Cloudy, later clearing.

HEXAGRAM 60

CHIEH

jie

Limitation

Primary	Upper	K'an	Abysmal
	Lower	Tui	Joyous
Nuclear	Above	Ken	Keeping Still
	Below	Chen	Arousing

Chieh means regulation, restriction, and restraints. The upper trigram *K'an* symbolizes water and the lower trigram *Tui* symbolizes marshes. The image is of a marsh receiving water. When too much water is received, the marsh will overflow; when too little water is received, the marsh will dry up. Thus, in receiving water, the marsh needs control and regulation. The appearance of the hexagram is likened to bamboo. In order from the bottom, lines one and two are solid or *yang* lines, lines three and four are broken or *yin* lines, line five is *yang*, and line six is *yin*. The alternation resembles the regulated joints on bamboo, hence strengthening the idea of uniformity and regulation. In divination, it means that one must do his duty, have self-control, and be content in his present position. Avoid greed and covetousness. Broken regulations and unrestraint and disorder will necessarily result in hardship, poverty, or difficulties.

THE FORTUNE

Be prudent, discriminating, and controlled in handling affairs. Greed or rash and forced actions must be avoided. Safe and sound smooth fortunes can be had if one is restrained and circumspect. Disregard of the principle of order and restraint and chaotic actions stemming from intoxication in pleasure and profit will result in loss, failure, and misfortune. In business, expenses may be too great. Financial difficulties. Things will not proceed smoothly. Careless words, rumors, or slander may cause injury.

Wish: No hope for the moment. Wait for a more opportune time.

Marriage: A good match. There is no need for anxiety or impetuousness. Patient and steady advance will lead to success.

Love: Success or failure will depend on the degree of patience.

Family: Orderly and sound household enjoying good fortune.

Children: Obedient and loyal; a happy family. But if the parents act immorally or in an improper fashion, the children will resist and the good fortune will be broken. Pregnancy: boy.

Capital loan: No hope for the time being.

Business: Just so-so.

Stock market: Only a slight fluctuation in prices.

Life span: If there is regimen and self-discipline, good health and long life will follow.

Sickness: Lengthy, but recovery is possible. Intake of food and drink must be regulated. Afflictions of the nervous system, stomach, and bowels.

Waiting for someone: Will not come for a while. Wait patiently.

Looking for someone: Nearby but whereabouts not easily discovered. Do not worry. This person's whereabouts will become known or he will return on his own.

Lost article: Lost indoors. Patient searching will lead to success. Search to the west or north.

Travel: Now is not a suitable time to go on a trip. Best wait for a more opportune moment.

Lawsuit and disputes: Adversity. Best seek a compromise.

Employment: No hope for the moment.

Examination: Fairly good score.

New business, change of occupation or specialization, and moving: Not the right time. Wait for a certain period and then look at the new situation.

Weather: Cloudy with occasional rain.

CHUNG FU

zhong fu

Inner truth

Primary	Upper	Sun	Gentle
	Lower	Tui	Joyous
Nuclear	Above	Ken	Keeping Still
	Below	Chen	Arousing

Chung Fu means sincerity and truth. The upper trigram *Sun* symbolizes the wind while the lower trigram *Tui* symbolizes marshes. The image is of wind blowing across the surface of a marsh, causing the water of the marsh to rise up and form waves. Thus it is likened to a superior treating subordinates with truth and sincerity, causing them to move in harmony, performing their functions and following willingly. *Tui* also represents joy and delight while *Sun* stands for obedience and following. The hexagram thus depicts happy and obedient compliance, the total lack of falsity and pretense, and mutual feeling and responsiveness. In divination, it means that sincerity, honesty, and truth in the conduct of affairs will mean the opening up of good fortune and smooth going.

THE FORTUNE

Handle all affairs with truth and sincerity, obtain the trust of others, and fortunes will gradually open up. Evil intentions and disregard of trust will

lead to bad fortune. In dealing with others pay particular attention to trust and good rewards can be had. Cooperative ventures are auspicious. The possibility exists of frequent trips outside.

Wish: Act with sincerity and it can be realized. Lack of sincerity will lead to failure.

Marriage: Good, compatible match. Success possible.

Love: In the midst of passionate love. Sincerity will now lead to success.

Family: Enjoying happiness and well being in harmony.

Children: Harmony between parents and children—happiness and well-being. Pregnancy: girl.

Capital loan: Smooth going.

Business: Smooth going. Moderate profits possible.

Stock market: Prices soon to rise.

Life span: Pay attention to the care of the body and a long life can be had.

Sickness: Recovery possible. Stomach swellings, peritonitis, and kidney afflictions.

Waiting for someone: Will definitely come.

Looking for someone: Do not worry. This person will voluntarily return soon.

Lost article: Lost indoors or has fallen into someone's hands. This person will return it.

Travel: Propitious. Safe and sound journey.

Lawsuit and disputes: Stubborn contention will result in adversity. Best to compromise.

Employment: Smooth going.

Examination: Very good score.

New business, change of occupation or specialization, and moving: Proceed, but do not force it.

Weather: Clear, later cloudy.

HSIAO KUO

xiao guo

Preponderance of the small

	Primary	Upper	Chen	Arousing
		Lower	Ken	Keeping Still
	Nuclear	Above	Tui	Joyous
		Below	Sun	Gentle

Hsiao Kuo means slight excess, disharmony, and trouble. The third and fourth lines from the bottom are solid or *yang* lines. The rest are broken or *yin* lines. The *yang* force is not in the seat of control. Moreover, it is surrounded by the *yin* force and cannot be brought into full play, suffering instead from slight troubles. *Yin* symbolizes smallness and *yang* largeness. The middle line, the controlling line of each trigram, is a *yin* line. Therefore it suggests that while small things can be accomplished there is no hope for accomplishing large things. The shape of the hexagram has the appearance of two people sitting with their backs to each other, thereby suggesting disharmony. In divination, it implies that things will not go very smoothly. One should keep within his sphere and not try to expand or advance.

THE FORTUNE

There is no hope of doing something outside the scope of one's abilities. Be especially careful not to quarrel with those whose strength or resources are very different, for this will lead to failure. Restraint and maintenance of the status quo are auspicious. Advancement is unfavorable. Disharmony may lead to involvement in complications. Separation from relatives and close friends is possible, as is committing a blunder in work.

Wish: Only a very small chance of success. Large wishes cannot be realized.

Marriage: Ill-suited match, incompatible, and leading to separation. Best to carefully reconsider.

Love: No success for a while. But too long a delay will end in failure, for the other party may have a change of heart.

Family: Disharmony in the family, fortunes declining. There is the possibility of leaving your native place and making a living outside.

Children: Disharmony between parents and children and among the children themselves. Pregnancy: boy.

Capital loan: Only small, not large, amount possible.

Business: Loss and failure.

Stock market: Prices low. Will make a jump upwards later but then drop once more.

Life span: Weak, subject to frequent sickness; a short life is a possibility.

Sickness: Will worsen. Extreme attention must be paid for recovery to be possible. Diabetes and chest afflictions.

Waiting for someone: Will not come.

Looking for someone: Far away and cannot be found.

Lost article: Stolen or lost and cannot be recovered.

Travel: Not favorable

Lawsuit and disputes: Adversity. Best stop.

Employment: No hope.

Examination: Poor score.

New business, change of occupation or specialization, and moving: Adversity. Best wait for another moment.

Weather: Cloudy in the morning and evening but clear around noon.

CHI CHI

ji ji

After completion

Primary	Upper	K'an	Abysmal
	Lower	Li	Clinging
Nuclear	Above	Li	Clinging
	Below	K'an	Abysmal

Chi Chi means everything is complete or already accomplished—after completion. The *yang* force symbolizes odd numbers and the *yin* even numbers. The lines alternate throughout the hexagram, one solid or *yang* line and then one broken or *yin* line. Each line is in its proper position and the two forces mutually succeed each other. The upper trigram *K'an* symbolizes the middle son while the lower trigram *Li* the middle daughter. The man and woman are in their proper places, suggesting suitable union. In divination, it means that now is the time for success and fame. But this moment will not last long and one must take precautions to prevent a decline in fortunes.

THE FORTUNE

Carefree, flourishing fortunes. There will be accomplishments, but as the fortune is at an extreme, signs of decline will appear. Therefore one must be neither arrogant nor negligent. Prudence and caution are a must for the good fortune to be maintained. Do not make plans for new developments. Maintain the present position, putting all things in order. There is a chance for momentary smooth going with the good fortune failing later.

Wish: Can be achieved but do not be careless.

Marriage: Smooth success. Well-suited match.

Love: Success possible. However, change will come if there is too long a delay. Better get married soon.

Family: Born in a family with flourishing fortunes. Blessings when young but fortunes will decline later.

Children: Blessings and happiness at first but later disharmony may appear between parents and children. Thus it is best for parents and children not to live with each other. Pregnancy: boy.

Capital loan: Success possible.

Business: Profits possible, but to seek excessive profits will result in failure.

Stock market: Rising prices. But be careful, for prices will fall after a few days.

Life span: Heretofore healthy and strong but after maturity health problems may arise. Therefore, take care of your body.

Sickness: Recovery is possible, but beware of a relapse. Heart ailments, diseases of the abdominal region, and diseases of the aged.

Waiting for someone: Will come.

Looking for someone: Will return voluntarily soon or whereabouts will become known. But this person may leave again.

Lost article: Can be found.

Travel: Safe and sound, but be careful en route.

Lawsuit and disputes: At first it will appear as though benefits or advantages can be gained, but this will later change for the worse, resulting in disadvantage. Best stop.

Employment: Success possible.

Examination: Good score.

New business, change of occupation or specialization, and moving: Best not to proceed. Reconsider.

Weather: Unstable weather.

HEXAGRAM 64

WEI CHI

wei ji

Before completion

Primary	*Upper*	*Li*	*Clinging*
	Lower	*K'an*	*Abysmal*
Nuclear	*Above*	*K'an*	*Abysmal*
	Below	*Li*	*Clinging*

Wei Chi means before completion, not yet accomplished, and before the outcome, result, or end. The upper trigram *Li* symbolizes fire while the lower trigram *K'an* stands for water. Fire burns upward and water flows downward. But here fire is above the water, meaning that both fire and water cannot act together or be mutually useful. Therefore, nothing is accomplished or completed. In divination, it means that fortunes are not now for the best but will be gradually changing for the better.

THE FORTUNE

Not smooth; nothing will go as hoped. Be calm, proceed steadily and gradually, get along with people harmoniously, and the fortune will by degrees improve. Being careless, rash, or negligent in conducting affairs will result in failure. Cooperative ventures are auspicious.

Wish: Difficulties. Hopeless for the moment. Continue striving and after a while success can be realized.

Marriage: At first the going will not be easy. Gradually both parties will come to a mutual understanding and success will follow. It is a good match.

Love: At first not too compatible but gradually will develop and result in success.

Family: At first difficulties and stagnant fortunes. Later the fortunes will gradually develop and the family members will, little by little, enjoy happiness and well-being. There is a possibility that the power or authority in the family is wielded by the wife.

Children: Toil and even distress because of the children at first. Later happiness and blessings will be reaped. Children may come late. Pregnancy: boy.

Capital loan: No hope for the time being.

Business: Losses. Later the situation will turn for the better.

Stock market: Falling prices.

Life span: Weak and sickly when young but will become healthy after maturity.

Sickness: Recovery after a long period of illness. Afflictions of the abdominal region or diseases of the blood and organs of circulation—veins, arteries, etc.

Waiting for someone: Probably will not come. But if this person does come, he will come late.

Looking for someone: Will take a long time but this person can be found. Look in the south or north.

Lost article: Patient searching will lead to success. The article has been misplaced in something. Search in the north or south.

Travel: Toilsome, not very smooth going.

Lawsuit and disputes: Time-consuming and not necessarily beneficial. Outcome unclear at present. A compromise is suggested.

Employment: For the time being no hope.

Examination: Poor or just so-so score.

New business, change of occupation or specialization, and moving: Proceed. Propitious.

Weather: Cloudy.

Bibliography

I-Ching Translations

Blofeld, John. *The Book of Change: A New Translation of the Ancient Chinese I-Ching (Yi-King)*. London: Allen and Unwin, 1965. New York: E. P. Dutton, 1968.
A simplified version with instructions for practical use of the *I-Ching* in divination.

Chai, Ch'u and Chai, Winberg, eds. *I-Ching: Book of Changes*. New Hyde Park: University Books, 1964. New York: Bantam Books, 1964.
The Legge translation with an introduction by the Chais explaining the structure of the *I-Ching*, its fundamental concepts, and philosophical concepts. A study guide is also provided.

The I-Ching Translated by James Legge. 2nd edition. New York: Dover Publications, 1963.
This is a reissue of the Legge translation.

Legge, James, trans. "The *Yi-King*," Pt. 2, *The Sacred Books of China*, *The Texts of Confucianism*. Sacred Books of the East, edited by F. Max Muller, vol. 16. Oxford: Clarendon, 1882. 2nd ed. 1899.
This translation by the great missionary-scholar became the most widely accepted English one until Richard Wilhelm's German was rendered into English.

Legge includes a lengthy introduction discussing the history of the *I-Ching* and the subject matter of the text and of the appendices. The translation is copiously annotated. It has been reprinted and reissued numerous times and has also served as the basis of several more recent translations.

Sung, Z. D., ed. *The Text of Yi-King*. (Reprint of the Shanghai 1935 edition) New York: Paragon Books, 1969.
The Legge translation with the Chinese text added.

Van Over, Raymond, ed. *I-Ching*. New York: Mentor Books, New American Library, 1971.
This is based on the Legge translation and has an introduction by the editor.

Wilhelm, Richard, trans. *The I-Ching or Book of Changes*. English translation by Cary F. Baynes, 3rd ed. Bollingen Series 19. Princeton: Princeton University Press, 1961.
Commonly referred to as the "Wilhelm-Baynes translation," this is now the most accepted and highly acclaimed translation in existence. In preparing his German translation in the second decade of this century, Wilhelm worked with China's most eminent scholars and relied principally on Lao Nai-hsüan. He checked his work by translating his German back into Chinese. C. G. Jung asked Baynes to do the English translation. And finally, Hellmut Wilhelm, the translator's son and a recognized authority on the *I-Ching* in his own right, checked the final proofs.
This work contains a foreword by C. G. Jung and a lengthy introduction by Richard Wilhelm explaining the use of the book, its history, and the arrangement

of the translation. Wilhelm has added elucidative remarks throughout and has appended an essay called "The Structure of the Hexagrams" to Book II. This edition has a special foreword by Hellmut Wilhelm and an appendix by the translator called "On Consulting the Oracle."

Articles and Papers on I-Ching

Chen, Shi-chuan. "How to Form a Hexagram and Consult the *I Ching*." *Journal of the American Oriental Society* 92, no. 2, pp. 237–49, 1972.

McEvilly, Wayne. "Synchronicity and the *I Ching*." *Philosophy East and West* 18, no. 3,   pp. 137–49, July 1968.

Needham, Joseph. "The System of the Book of Changes," in *Science and Civilization in China* by J. Needham and Wang Ling. History of Scientific Thought, vol. 2, pp. 304–45. Cambridge: At the University Press, 1956.

Swanson, Gerald William. "The Great Treatise: Commentary Tradition to the Book of Changes." Ph.D. dissertation, University of Washington, 1974.

Van der Blij, F. "Combinational Aspects of the Hexagrams in the Chinese Book of Changes." *Scripta Mathematica* 28, no. 1, pp. 37–49, 1966.

Wilhelm, Hellmut. "The Concept of Time in the Book of Changes." Translated by Ralph Manheim. Papers from the Eranos Yearbooks, Bollingen Series 30, edited by Joseph Campbell, vol. 3, *Man and Time*, pp. 212–324. New York: Pantheon Books, 1957.

———. "The Creative Principle in the Book of Changes." Translated by Jane A. Pratt and Marianne Cowan. *Spring 1970*.

———. "Interplay of Image and Concept in the Book of Changes." *Eranos Jahrbuch 1967*, 36. Zurich: Rhein-Verlag, 1968.

———. "The Sacrifice, Idea and Attitude: Thoughts from the Book of Changes." *Harvest*, vol. 4 (1957). Reprinted under the title "On Sacrifice in the *I Ching*." *Spring 1972*.

Secondary Sources of Information about *I-Ching*

Cage, John. *Silence: Lectures and Writings*. Middletown, Connecticut: Wesleyan University Press, 1961.

Culling, Louis T. *The Incredible I Ching*. New York: Weiser, 1969.

Da Liu. *I Ching Coin Prediction*. New York and Evanston: Harper and Row, 1975

Hook, Diana. *The I-Ching and You*. New York: Dutton, 1973.

Johnson, Willard. *I Ching: An Introduction to the Book of Changes*. Berkeley: Shambala, 1969.

Lee, Chin, and Wong, Kay. *I Ching Book of Change*. Tujunga, California: The K. King Company, 1971.

Lee, Yung Young. *The Principles of Changes: Understanding the I Ching*. New Hyde Park: University Books, 1971.

McCaffree, Joe E. *Divination and the Historical and Allegorical Sources of the I Ching, the Chinese Classic or Book of Changes*. Los Angeles: Miniverse Services, 1967.

Murphy, Joseph. *Secrets of the I Ching*. West Nyack, New York: Parker, 1970.

Ponce, Charles. *The Nature of the I Ching: Its Usage and Interpretation*. New York: Award Books, 1970.

Sung, Z. D. *The Symbols of Yi-King or the Symbols of the Chinese Logic of Changes*. (Reprint of the Shanghai 1934 ed.) New York: Paragon, 1969.

Sze, Mai-Mai. *The Tao of Painting: A Study of the Ritual Disposition of Chinese Painting*. Bollingen Series 49. New York: Pantheon Books, 1956.

Wilhelm, Hellmut. *Change: Eight Lectures on the I Ching*. Translated from the German by Cary F. Baynes. Bollingen Series 62. New York: Pantheon Books, 1960. New York: Harper Torchbooks, 1964. Princeton: Princeton University Press, 1973.

Woo, Catherine Yi-yu Cho. *Characters of the Hexagrams of the I Ching*. San Diego: University Press, California State University, 1972.